Persons and
Personal Identity

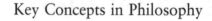

Key Concepts in Philosophy

Guy Axtell, *Objectivity*
Heather Battaly, *Virtue*
Lisa Bortolotti, *Irrationality*
Joseph Keim Campbell, *Free Will*
Roy T. Cook, *Paradoxes*
Douglas Edwards, *Properties*
Ian Evans and Nicholas D. Smith, *Knowledge*
Bryan Frances, *Disagreement*
Douglas Kutach, *Causation*
Carolyn Price, *Emotion*
Darrell P. Rowbottom, *Probability*
Daniel Speak, *The Problem of Evil*
Matthew Talbert, *Moral Responsibility*
Deborah Perron Tollefsen, *Groups as Agents*
Joshua Weisberg, *Consciousness*
Chase Wrenn, *Truth*

Persons and Personal Identity

Amy Kind

polity

First published in 2015 by Polity Press

Polity Press
65 Bridge Street
Cambridge CB2 1UR, UK

Polity Press
350 Main Street
Malden, MA 02148, USA

ISBN-13: 978-0-7456-5431-7
ISBN-13: 978-0-7456-5432-4 (pb)

A catalog record for this book is available from the British Library.

Library of Congress Cataloging-in-Publication Data

Kind, Amy.
    Persons and personal identity / Amy Kind.
        pages cm
    Includes bibliographical references and index.
        ISBN 978-0-7456-5431-7 (hardback : alk. paper) – ISBN 978-0-7456-5432-4
(pbk. : alk. paper)   1. Individualism.   2. Persons.   3. Identity
(Psychology)   I. Title.
    B824.K56 2015
    126–dc23

                                                                    2014046428

Typeset in 10.5 on 12 pt Sabon
by Toppan Best-set Premedia Limited
Printed and bound in the UK by CPI Group (UK) Ltd, Croydon

For further information on Polity, visit our website:
politybooks.com

Contents

Acknowledgements

I was first seriously introduced to issues about personal identity as an undergraduate in a class taught by Jyl Gentzler. As a graduate student, my thinking about persons and personal identity was further shaped by various classes and helpful conversations with professors such as Robert Adams, Joseph Almog, Keith Donnellan, Kit Fine, and Seana Shiffrin. I am grateful to all of them.

The Berger Institute at Claremont McKenna College (CMC) provided me with a summer research grant that facilitated some of my early work on this project. I greatly appreciate their support.

One of the joys of teaching at CMC has been to get to work closely with our excellent students. My thinking about persons and personal identity has been shaped over the years by students in various classes, perhaps most notably in the sections that I've taught of Metaphysics, Metaphysics of Persons, and Philosophy through Science Fiction. I am especially indebted to two CMC students in particular. First, this book would not have been possible without the help of my undergraduate research assistant Sara Stern. Not only did she conduct an extensive literature search for me at an early stage of this project, but she also synthesized her results in several insightful and beautifully compiled reports. Chapter 6 in particular was greatly influenced by her work. More recently, this book has benefitted from the careful comments and bibliographic attention provided by my undergraduate research assistant Jared Goldberg.

This book has been significantly improved by all of the feedback I've received along the way. Thanks go to my colleague Eric Yang for providing helpful comments on the entire draft manuscript. Thanks also go to the three anonymous referees who reviewed and made suggestions on my original proposal, and the two anonymous referees who reviewed the draft manuscript. I am especially grateful for the support of the Polity editorial team – and particularly Emma Hutchinson and Pascal Porcheron – throughout this project.

I dedicate this book to the three most important persons in my life, my husband Frank Menetrez, and my two sons, Stephen and Joseph.

The Nature of Persons

On the list of the world's most famous gorillas, King Kong probably takes the top spot. Right behind him in second place we might likely find Koko, an eastern lowland gorilla whose fame owes not to Hollywood – though she has been featured in several films – but rather to her prowess at American Sign Language. Since the age of one, Koko has been learning to sign as part of her participation in The Gorilla Language Project, a study led by developmental psychologist Francine Patterson that aims to gather information about the intelligence and linguistic capabilities of gorillas. Now in her forties, Koko reportedly has a working vocabulary of over 1,000 signs and understands approximately 2,000 spoken English words. According to her handlers, she exhibits self-awareness, a sense of humor, empathy, and a wide range of emotions. On IQ tests, she has scored between 70 and 95 (where a score of 100 is considered to be normal for humans). Demonstrating considerable linguistic creativity, Koko has created new signs, modified existing signs to extend their meanings, and combined signs in novel ways. To mention one such example that is especially interesting for our purposes here, she has referred to herself using sign language as a "fine gorilla person."

On the face of it, Koko's self-description might seem to be a contradiction in terms. In ordinary speech, we frequently take the term "person" to mean "human being" – member of the species *Homo sapiens* – and there can't possibly be any such thing as a gorilla human being, fine or not. But there's another sense of the word "person," one often employed in philosophical discussion, in which there is no contradiction in referring to a non-human individual as a person. Our interest in this chapter, and throughout this book as a whole, is in this latter sense. In the philosophical sense of personhood, the terms "person" and "human being" should not be taken to be synonymous, and it is at least conceptually possible both that there be non-human persons and that there be non-person humans. That's not yet to say that Koko is right to call herself a person – whether any existing non-humans should be considered persons (and if so, which) is a question that we'll consider later in section 1.3. But for now, what's important to note is that the issue is not settled simply as a matter of definition. Although we can specify what a human being is in biological terms, we cannot give a similar biological specification of what a person is. The nature of persons is not something that can be revealed by genetic testing or other laboratory analysis.

Our inquiry into persons and personal identity throughout this book will be a *metaphysical* one. Metaphysics is the branch of philosophy that deals with the nature and structure of the world. It's perhaps easiest to understand the study of metaphysics by contrasting it with epistemology, another branch of philosophy. In epistemology, philosophers are concerned with the nature of knowledge and justification. We might ask, for example: What justifies the belief that God exists? Or: Can we have knowledge of God's existence? By contrast, in metaphysics, philosophers are concerned not with our knowledge of the world, but with the world itself. We thus might ask: Does God exist? Or: What is the nature of God?

There are many interesting epistemological questions about persons, prime among them the question of how an individual can know of the existence of any person other than herself. Perhaps I am the only person who exists, and the apparent persons around me are really just mindless automata. What justifies me in believing otherwise? (In philosophy of mind, questions of this sort are often discussed under the framework of the *problem of other minds*.) In this book, we'll put these epistemological questions aside to focus on meta-physical questions about persons. We'll focus on three questions in particular:

- *The identification question:* What properties must a being have to count as a person?
- *The reidentification question:* What makes a person the same person over time?
- *The characterization question:* What makes a person the person that she is?

It is probably not surprising that there is considerable philosophical disagreement about how these questions should be answered. What may be more surprising is that there is also considerable disagreement about how these questions should be properly formulated and how they are related to one another – in fact, there is even disagreement about *whether* they are related to one another. As we take up these questions over the course of the book, we will see how these disagreements come into play. We start, however, with the identification question.

1.1 Notions of Personhood

In exploring the properties necessary for a thing to count as a person, the target of our investigation in this first chapter is what's often referred to as *metaphysical personhood*. Unfortunately, this is not the only notion of personhood in play in philosophical discussion. Philosophers talk not only of metaphysical personhood but also of moral personhood, and they are not always careful to distinguish the two. Moreover, the notion of personhood plays a central role in many legal systems. Thus, before we can begin our inquiry into metaphysical personhood, we need first to disentangle these various notions.

The notion of person has always been of central importance to Western legal systems. Consider, for example, the all-important due process and equal protection clauses of the Fourteenth Amendment of the United States Constitution: "[No State shall] deprive any person of life, liberty, or property, without due process of law; nor deny to any person within its jurisdiction the equal protection of the laws." To be a person before the law – to be a *legal person* – is to be the subject of legal rights and obligations. But who counts as a person in this sense?

First, it's clear that being human is not itself sufficient for being a legal person. At various times, and in various societies, legal personhood has been denied to classes of human beings such as women and slaves. British law prior to the middle of the nineteenth century did not recognize married women as legal persons. As explained by Sir William Blackstone in his famous eighteenth-century *Commentaries on the Laws of England*, "By marriage, the husband and wife are one person in law: that is, the very being or legal existence of the woman is suspended during the marriage, or at least is incorporated and consolidated into that of the husband." In the United States, the Supreme Court ruled in the infamous Dred Scott case of 1857 that the US Constitution considered slaves to be property, not persons. In recent decades, the notion of legal personhood has been a hotly contested issue with respect to human fetuses. Ruling on this issue in *Roe* v. *Wade*, the Supreme Court declared that the word "person" as used in the Fourteenth Amendment does not apply to the unborn.

Second, it's also clear that being human fails to be necessary for being a legal person. Perhaps the most obvious example stems from the granting of legal personhood to corporations. In the United States, the Supreme Court ruled in the nineteenth century that corporations were explicitly declared to be legal persons in the sense of the Fourteenth Amendment. Given that a corporation consists of a collection of human beings, this declaration might not seem to fully sever the link between being human and being a legal person, but there are also numerous examples of legal systems having granted personhood to inanimate objects such as temples, church buildings, and ships. Moreover, in recent years, legal scholars have contemplated whether we might appropriately extend legal personhood to the great apes (Francione 1993), computer systems with artificial intelligence (Solum 2008), and natural objects such as forests, rivers, and oceans (Stone 1972). In a historic ruling in late 2014, an Argentinean appeals court recognized Sandra, a captive orangutan, as a non-human person who accordingly has the basic right of bodily autonomy. As a result of the ruling, Sandra will be transferred from the Buenos Aires zoo to an animal sanctuary.

As this suggests, an entity might be a legal person relative to one legal system yet not a legal person relative to another. Whether a given entity counts as a legal person does not depend solely on the entity's nature but rather on facts about a given legal system. This sharply differentiates the notion of legal personhood from the notion of moral personhood, in which facts about the nature of the entity are taken to be paramount.

Generally speaking, when we say that an entity has moral personhood, we include it as part of our moral community and treat it as deserving of moral consideration. Sometimes moral personhood is identified specifically with having the right to life. In this way of viewing the notion, what it is for an entity to be a person in the moral sense is for it to have the right to life. More commonly, however, the notion of moral personhood is understood more broadly so that what it is for an entity to be a person in the moral sense is for it to be an agent with rights and responsibilities.

Suppose that Bill has come to visit his friend Jack and that, after a few too many drinks, Bill becomes increasingly belligerent for no apparent reason. First he picks up Jack's favorite lamp and smashes it to bits. Next he kicks Jack's cat. And finally he slaps Jack across the face. Clearly, each of these actions was wrong, and Bill is probably not going to be invited over again anytime soon. But while it was wrong to slap Jack *because it wrongs him*, and while I suspect that many of us would agree that it was wrong to kick the cat *because it wrongs the cat*, matters are different when it comes to the lamp. What makes the smashing of the lamp wrong was *not* that it wrongs the lamp. The fact that the lamp belongs to Jack, and that he values it, makes it unacceptable for Bill to smash it. But the lamp, lacking any interests of its own, cannot be morally wronged. It is not the kind of thing that can have any rights, and likewise, not the kind of thing to which we have any moral obligations. Unlike Jack and the cat, the lamp lacks moral status.

Treating both Jack and the cat as having moral status does not commit us to saying that the wrong done to Jack and the wrong done to the cat were on a par. There are all sorts of reasons that it might be worse to harm a human being than to harm a cat. For example, some philosophers have claimed that moral status – and hence moral personhood – comes in degrees, so perhaps a human has a fuller degree of moral personhood than a cat (see, e.g., Warren 1997). That said, it's also worth noting that not everyone agrees that a cat has any degree of moral personhood at all. Historically, this latter view has been closely associated with Immanuel Kant, an eighteenth-century German philosopher. On Kant's view, the cat, like the lamp, is a mere thing.

Our stance on issues of this kind depends on our account of moral personhood – that is, on what feature or set of features we think an entity has to have in order for it to be a moral person. Accounts of moral personhood attempt to specify its necessary and sufficient conditions. To say that a condition is *necessary* for moral personhood is to say that *all* entities counting as persons in the moral sense must have met that condition; meeting the condition is <u>required</u> for moral personhood. To say that a condition is *sufficient* for moral personhood is to say that *any* entities meeting that condition count as persons in the moral sense; meeting the condition is <u>enough</u> for moral personhood. Thus, a set of necessary and sufficient conditions for moral personhood specifies the conditions such that all and only entities meeting those conditions are moral persons.

What I'll call *species accounts* treat membership in a particular species – typically, the human species – to be both necessary and sufficient for personhood. Such views, which seem to have their roots in the Judeo-Christian tradition, are frequently defended on religious grounds. Often cited in this context is the following biblical passage from the book of Genesis:

> God created man in His own image, in the image of God created He him; male and female created He them. And God blessed them, and God said unto them, "Be fruitful and multiply, and replenish the earth, and subdue it; and have dominion over the fish of the sea, and over the fowl of the air, and

over every living thing that moveth upon the earth." (Genesis 1:27–1:28, American Standard Version)

This passage seems to suggest two different considerations relevant to the defense of species accounts: (1) humans have special moral status because they (and only they) are made in God's image; and (2) humans have special moral status because God gave them dominion over the animals. Species accounts have been subject to considerable criticism in contemporary discussion of moral personhood. Apart from a theological justification – i.e., apart from simply taking it to be true as a matter of religious faith – it is difficult to see how such an account could be defended. Moreover, many philosophers have charged that a focus on species seems as arbitrary as a focus on race or sex or nationality. For example, Australian philosopher Peter Singer, whose 1975 book *Animal Liberation* has been extremely influential in the fight for animal rights, argues as follows:

> Racists violate the principle of equality by giving greater weight to the interests of members of their own race when there is a clash between their interests and the interests of those of another race. Sexists violate the principle of equality by favoring the interests of their own sex. Similarly, speciesists allow the interests of their own species to override the greater interests of members of other species. The pattern is identical in each case. (Singer 1975/1990, 9)

When we condemn racism and sexism, we do so because the focus on characteristics such as skin color or gender are irrelevant to one's moral standing. How could those be features that make a difference? The criticism of speciesism is parallel. How could the mere fact that one is a member of one species rather than another be relevant to one's moral standing? The fact that we are members of the species *Homo sapiens* – as opposed, say, to the species *Felis catus* or *Giraffa camelopardalis* – just identifies the particular group of living organisms with which we are capable of breeding so as to produce fertile offspring.

In response to these criticisms, some defenders of species accounts have dug in their heels. For example, American philosopher Carl Cohen not only identifies himself as a speciesist but also insists that speciesism is essential for correct moral reasoning. Dismissing the analogy between speciesism and racism as "insidious," Cohen claims that while there are no morally relevant distinctions between members of different races, there are morally relevant distinctions between members of different species. Unlike, say, cats or giraffes, humans engage in moral reflection, are morally autonomous, are members of moral communities, and recognize just claims against their own interest (Cohen 1986).

Interestingly, however, this sort of defense of speciesism seems to undercut itself. The invocation of features such as the capacity for reflection and autonomy suggests that it's not species membership in and of itself that matters, but rather the fact that being a member of the species *Homo sapiens* tends to go along with the possession of certain features. But as we will discuss in more detail below, not all members of the human species have the capacity for reflection and autonomy (e.g., the severely cognitively impaired) and there may be members of other species that do. And the problem here is not just with the particular features that Cohen has picked out. More generally, it's hard to see how one could come up with a list of such features that would apply to all and only human beings. Thus, either one is back to the claim that species itself is all that matters – in which case the charge of speciesism again seems to have bite – or one has really switched to a different kind of account, one in which moral personhood consists in the possession of certain features.

Since the features that tend to be discussed in this context are mental in nature, this latter kind of account is what I'll call a *mental capacity account* of moral personhood. On this kind of view, what matters for moral personhood is not what species you belong to but rather what psychological attributes you have. Most accounts of moral personhood on offer in contemporary philosophical discussions are mental capacity accounts, although there is considerable disagreement about how exactly to specify the relevant mental capacity or capacities. Is it consciousness? Self-consciousness? Rationality? Autonomy? Sentience? Or some combination thereof? To give just a few examples of how such accounts have been developed:

- Mary Anne Warren marks out five traits as central to the notion of moral personhood: consciousness, the capacity of reasoning, being capable of self-motivated activity, having the capacity to communicate, and having the presence of self-concepts and self-awareness (Warren 1973).
- Michael Tooley defines moral personhood in terms of self-consciousness. In order for an entity to be a moral person, it must be a subject of experiences and be aware of itself as a subject of experiences (Tooley 1983).
- Daniel Dennett offers six conditions that he thinks are necessary for moral personhood: (1) persons are rational beings; (2) persons are beings whose behavior can be explained and predicted in terms of intentional states, i.e., states like beliefs, desires, hopes, fears, intentions, perceptions, expectations, and so on; (3) for an entity to be a person, a certain stance must be adopted with respect to it; in other words, "our treating him or her or it in this certain way is somehow and to some extent constitutive of its being a person" (Dennett 1976, 178); (4) the entity must be capable of reciprocating this stance in some way; (5) persons must be capable of verbal communication; and (6) persons are conscious in some special way, perhaps by being self-conscious.
- Tom Regan focuses on what he calls *being the subject-of-a-life*. Being the subject-of-a-life requires an entity to

> have beliefs and desires; perception, memory, a sense of the future, including their own future; an emotional life together with feelings of pleasure and pain; preference- and welfare-interests; the ability to initiate action in pursuit of their desires and goals; a psychophysical identity over time; and an individual welfare in the sense that their experiential life fares well or ill for them, logically independent of their being the object of anyone else's interests. (Regan 2004, 243)

As we will see, mental capacities also feature centrally in discussions of metaphysical personhood. I will thus postpone further discussion of them until section 1.2 when we take up this notion in detail. But before we conclude our discussion of moral personhood, it will be useful to make explicit two important general facts about mental capacity accounts:

first, that they leave open the possibility that there could be non-human moral persons, and second, that they leave open the possibility that not all humans are moral persons.

While it is not clear that animals such as cats and dogs will meet all the requirements laid out above, there are other mammals such as dolphins and the great apes that might. (The mental capacities of animals such as dolphins and apes will be discussed in more detail below in section 1.3.) We can also imagine all sorts of alien races that meet these requirements – from Wookiees like Chewbacca to Hobbits like Bilbo Baggins. In fact, we can even imagine machines that meet the specifications of mental capacity accounts. Consider Andrew, the sentient robot in Isaac Asimov's *Bicentennial Man*, or Data, the android Starfleet officer of *Star Trek: The Next Generation*, both of whom seem to possess many of the relevant mental capacities. Thus, if mental capacity accounts are correct, not only does it fail to matter what species you are, but also it doesn't even matter whether you're biologically alive.

But mental capacity accounts also tend to exclude many humans from the class of moral persons. Newborn infants, for example, don't yet have many of the mental capacities listed above. Some of these capacities also seem absent in individuals with congenital brain damage who are significantly cognitively impaired, or individuals in persistent vegetative states. Of course, even if such individuals are excluded from the class of moral persons, that is not to imply that they can be indiscriminately killed. But it does suggest that an analysis of why it would be wrong to kill such individuals would have to rely on indirect reasons, not reasons relating to the moral personhood of the individuals themselves.

This unpalatable consequence has suggested to some contemporary philosophers that mental capacity accounts are misguided, and they have correspondingly offered various alternative accounts. Many of these alternatives can be grouped together as versions of what I'll call *relational accounts*. According to such accounts, the problem with mental capacity accounts stems not from focusing on the wrong sorts of capacities but from focusing on capacities at all. The problem is that capacities are *intrinsic* properties of individuals. Roughly speaking, an intrinsic property is one that an individual has in and of itself, a property that it would have even if it were the only thing in the world. But it might naturally be thought that our moral rights and duties to one another arise at least based in part on our relationships to one another. Building on this idea, relational accounts claim that an individual's moral personhood derives at least in part from the individual's place in a complex web of social and interpersonal relationships. Newborns and individuals with brain damage, even if they lack certain intrinsic mental capacities, stand in these kinds of relationships and thus are not ruled out as persons in the moral sense.

As this brief discussion suggests, figuring out the right account of moral personhood is a very tricky business, with conflicting intuitions often pulling us in different directions. In fact, the difficulty has led some philosophers to treat the very notion of moral personhood with suspicion and to suggest that we abandon the search for a proper account of it. As Jane English has argued, "There is no single core of necessary and sufficient features which we can draw upon with the assurance that they constitute what really makes a person; there are only features that are more or less typical" (English 2005, 234–5). Likewise, Tom Beauchamp has suggested that our concept of person "is simply not orderly, precise, or systematic in a way that supports one general philosophical theory to the exclusion of another" (Beauchamp 1999, 319).

maybe we will never have a true, definitive concept of a person

Despite such skepticism, however, discussion of moral personhood continues to play a key role in debates about a wide array of social practices and public policies – from disputes about abortion, euthanasia, and physician-assisted suicide to those about factory farming and vegetarianism. It should thus come as no surprise that discussion of moral personhood is often fraught with tension. Fortunately, it is not our purpose here to adjudicate this issue. Our interest in moral personhood stems primarily from the need to distinguish it from metaphysical personhood.

As we have seen, legal and moral personhood are *normative* or *evaluative* notions. To ascribe legal personhood to an entity is to say that it has a certain legal status, i.e., that it has certain legal rights. To ascribe moral personhood to an entity is to say that it has a certain moral status, i.e., that it has certain moral rights. But the ascription of legal or moral personhood to an entity does not thereby tell us anything about what kind of thing it is or what properties it has. In contrast, metaphysical personhood is a *descriptive* notion. In ascribing metaphysical personhood to an entity we thereby provide at least a partial description of it.

Of course, it seems plausible that moral and metaphysical personhood are very closely connected. Perhaps such notions even perfectly coincide, such that all and only persons in the metaphysical sense are persons in the moral sense. But this result would not show that the two notions are the same. To use a familiar philosophical example, it turns out that all and only creatures that have a heart are creatures with kidneys – having a circulatory system requires both a pump (the heart) and a waste removal system (the kidneys). But the notion "creature with a heart" is different from that of "creature with a kidney"; the first phrase has a different meaning from the second phrase.

In what follows, we'll proceed under the assumption that metaphysical personhood and moral personhood are, likewise, distinct notions. Not everyone agrees with this assumption. For example, after developing his account of moral personhood, Dennett claims that the metaphysical and moral notions of personhood "are not separate and distinct concepts but just two different and unstable resting points on the same continuum" (Dennett 1976, 193). But given that inquiries in metaphysics generally aim for non-normative descriptions of the fundamental features of reality, it seems worthwhile to try to keep the metaphysical notion of person separate from the moral notion of person.

One might worry that the separation of metaphysical personhood from moral personhood deprives it of any real interest. If our inquiry into the notion of metaphysical personhood will not shed light on how such a being should be treated, or on whether we owe it moral consideration, then perhaps there is not much point to it. As might be expected, however, I think such a worry is misguided. First, a notion of metaphysical personhood that's wholly distinct from the notion of moral personhood might well be of considerable use in attempting to construct an account of moral personhood. But second, and in my view more importantly, the notion of metaphysical personhood has importance in its own right. What could be more interesting, more important, than achieving a deeper understanding of ourselves, and of what kind of beings we fundamentally are?

1.2   Metaphysical Personhood

Consider a non-disabled adult human being. Such a being is undoubtedly a person in the metaphysical sense, if anything is. What are some other examples of persons in the metaphysical sense? There are various sorts of candidates we might consider:

- human beings in different life-stages
- human beings with various disabilities
- non-human mammals
- other animals
- single-celled organisms
- alien beings
- non-organic beings
- non-physical beings

Many of these candidates undoubtedly belong to the class of metaphysical persons, while some undoubtedly do not. In some cases, the answer is not clear cut. This might be because we need more information: What kind of animal is it? What kind of alien? What capacities does it have? But it also might be because our intuitions about metaphysical personhood are still somewhat muddled. The discussion of this section aims to sharpen those intuitions. In doing so, I will usually drop the qualifiers "metaphysical" and "in the metaphysical sense" – references to persons and personhood from here on should be understood to be picking out metaphysical persons and metaphysical personhood.

In Hollywood, in Madame Tussaud's wax museum, there is a wax replica of the actor Johnny Depp. The replica looks remarkably like Johnny Depp himself, enough for you perhaps to be fooled for a moment or two, before the complete lack of motion made you suspicious. The wax replica of Johnny

Depp is clearly not a person. But Johnny Depp clearly is. So the first point to note – one that should be completely uncontroversial – is that having a characteristic human appearance is not sufficient for something to be a person.

appearance is ∅ enough to be a person

Having a characteristic human appearance also is not necessary for something to be a person. Even many human beings don't have a characteristic human appearance. In 1999, when the car in which she was riding was hit by a drunk driver, Jacqueline Saburido was engulfed by flames. Suffering burns over 60 percent of her body, she lost her hair, ears, nose, lips, and left eyelid. All of her fingers had to be amputated. But her personhood isn't in doubt. In 2013, the Pope embraced an unidentified man with no facial features at all. Once again, that man's personhood isn't in doubt. Even being of humanoid form is not necessary for something to be a person. If an alien race resembling giant bugs were to land on earth, their insect-like appearance would not count against the possibility of their being persons. Likewise, the facts that dolphins have flippers and gorillas have fur don't count against the possibility of their being persons either. Maybe they're persons, maybe they're not – but the fact that they don't look like human beings isn't relevant. When it comes to personhood, an entity's physical form plays no role.

But this raises a natural question: Must a person have physical form at all? Here matters are not quite as clear. The twentieth-century philosopher P. F. Strawson claimed that the concept of person "is the concept of a type of entity such that *both* predicates ascribing states of consciousness *and* predicates ascribing corporeal characteristics" can be equally applied (1959, 101–2). On the other hand, many religious traditions take God to be a person, and angels are treated as persons as well. The iOS personal assistant Siri, who explicitly declines to discuss her existential status, probably isn't a person, but what about the advanced operating system depicted in Spike Jonze's 2013 movie *Her*? Samantha has many of the qualities that persons typically have, and she interacts with her human companions in a person-like manner, despite lacking any physical presence.

The seventeenth-century English philosopher John Locke, whose discussion of this topic has been extremely influential in the philosophical literature, does not include reference to physical presence in his definition. On his view, a person is "a thinking intelligent being, that has reason and reflection, and can consider itself as itself, the same thinking thing in different times and places; which it does only by that consciousness, which is inseparable from thinking, and as it seems to me, essential to it: It being impossible for anyone to perceive, without perceiving that he does perceive" (Locke 1689/1975, 335). Locke was not the first to highlight the capacities for reason and reflection as central to the notion of person. More than a millennium earlier, the Roman philosopher Boethius had defined *person* as "the individual substance of a rational nature" (Boethius 1918, 85). But this view, in which the essence of personhood consists in the capacity for self-consciousness – in the ability for an entity to "consider itself as itself" – is generally associated with Locke.

It's hard to question the claim that self-consciousness is necessary for personhood. Consider Watson, the machine designed by researchers at IBM to compete on *Jeopardy!*. Powered by a system consisting of 10 server racks and 90 IBM Power 750 servers based on the POWER7 processor, Watson has computing power comparable to a super-high-speed network of more than 2,880 computers. In February 2011, Watson was matched up against two formidable human opponents: Ken Jennings, who holds the record for longest consecutive win streak on *Jeopardy!*, and Brad Rutter, three time *Jeopardy!* Tournament winner. The final score? Watson: $77,147; Jennings: $24,000; Rutter: $21,600. But while Watson has many extremely impressive traits – factual knowledge, strategical know-how, an ability to interpret complex and often ambiguous phrases – it lacks any kind of awareness of itself. In fact, it lacks any real understanding at all. Unsurprisingly, no one acquainted with it seems to feel any temptation to think of it as a person.

But is self-consciousness sufficient for personhood? Consider a being who can reflect on itself but can do nothing else. It has no capacity for memory, for planning, for learning, for communicating, and so on. It's hard to get a sense of what such a being is like, but it's also hard to think of a creature as limited as this as a person. For this reason, though many of the contemporary accounts of metaphysical personhood

Self-cons. Not enough either

that have been offered are in the Lockean tradition, most of them provide a more expansive set of necessary and sufficient conditions than Locke did. For example, Joel Feinberg and Barbara Baum Levenbook offer the following account: "Persons are those beings who, among other things, are conscious, have a concept and awareness of themselves, are capable of experiencing emotions, can reason and acquire understanding, can plan ahead, can act on their plans, and can feel pleasure and pain" (Feinberg and Levenbook 1992, 201).

Though Locke's definition might have seemed too narrow, the inclusion of some of these conditions might seem questionable. For example, suppose we encountered a being who had all the other traits specified but who was unable to experience pleasure and pain, and who lacked the capacity to experience emotion. Here we might again think of Data, the android Starfleet officer of the television series *Star Trek: The Next Generation*. While the Vulcans of *Star Trek* are often referred to as emotionless, that description is inaccurate. Vulcans have the capacity to experience emotions but simply repress them. Data, on the other hand, lacks this capacity. He also cannot feel pleasure and pain. Special technology – an emotion chip and skin grafts – eventually enables him to experience both emotions and bodily sensations. But let's consider him prior to those enhancements. He is sentient, intelligent, and self-aware. He can learn from his experiences, and he seeks out new knowledge. He can plan and act on his plans. He successfully maintains working relationships and friendships with other members of the *Enterprise* crew. It is hard to see why we would exclude him from the class of metaphysical persons based solely on the fact that he can experience neither emotion nor pleasure and pain.

Of course, Data is an example from science fiction, and, in real life, the ability to reason and the ability to experience emotion seem to go hand in hand. In recent years, psychologist Antonio Damasio has presented a persuasive case that emotions play a central role in reasoning. To make his case, Damasio considers real-world examples like that of Elliot, a man in his thirties who was discovered to have an orange-sized tumor growing in the midline area of his brain above the nasal cavities. After the tumor was removed via successful surgery, Elliott returned to good health, but he also underwent a radical change of personality. As Damasio recounts, though Elliott suffered no apparent defects of memory or understanding, he lost his ability to function in daily life: he was unable to manage his time and his decision-making became severely impaired. For example, if tasked with sorting files, he could spend an entire afternoon simply trying to decide upon a categorization system to use (by date? by file size? by topic?). Though Elliot was able to perform well on a vast array of cognitive tests, Damasio ultimately concluded that his problem stemmed from a severe emotional deficit. After the surgery, he was unable to experience emotion, and it was this that was the root of his troubles. As Damasio claims, "the cold-bloodedness of Elliot's reasoning prevented him from assigning different values to different options, and made his decision-making landscape hopelessly flat" (Damasio 1994, 51). Interestingly, however, even if Damasio is right, he would not have shown that emotions are essential for personhood. Even if an individual's capacity to reason (and hence to function in the everyday world) is severely attenuated in the absence of emotions, it does not disappear entirely. And though everyone who knew him thought that Elliot was significantly changed as a result of the surgery – as Damasio puts it, "Elliot was no longer Elliot" (Damasio 1994, 36) – no one seemed to think that he had lost his personhood altogether.

Other contemporary accounts in this general spirit offer slightly different lists from the one we've been considering from Feinberg and Levenbook. But it is also worth noting that some contemporary accounts of personhood lie outside the Lockean tradition. Perhaps the most influential such account is the one offered by Harry Frankfurt. On Frankfurt's view, what's essential for personhood is not self-consciousness but rather the capacity to exercise freedom of the will. Frankfurt's account involves several key notions and distinctions relating to desire and the will, so to understand his account, we need to fill in a bit of background.

Humans typically have all sorts of desires, both long-term and short-term. Right now I want all sorts of things: I want to have a productive day of work, I want to exercise more frequently, I want my kids to turn down the music they're listening to, and I want another Diet Coke. Humans are not unique in having desires; all sorts of creatures have them. Take my dog, for example. Sometimes he wants a tummy rub, sometimes he wants to greet the guests coming in the door, sometimes he wants to lie peacefully in the sun, and sometimes (in fact, often) he wants food. Humans are different from dogs, however, in that we not only have the sorts of desires mentioned above but also have desires about our desires. To use Frankfurt's terminology, in addition to our *first-order desires* we also have *second-order desires*. Not only do I want to exercise more frequently, but I want to have that desire. On the other hand, as I'm trying to meet a work-related deadline, my desire to spend the day at the beach is making it difficult to concentrate, and I wish I didn't have it. My dog, in contrast, does not care one way or the other about his desires; he just has them. Unlike me, he lacks this capacity for reflective self-evaluation.

Our first-order desires often pull us in different directions. My desire to sleep late conflicts with my desire to work out, and my desire to finish a writing project conflicts with my desire to spend the day at the beach. So not all of our desires move us to action. But when a first-order desire does move someone to action, when it is effective, that desire is what Frankfurt calls an agent's *will*. Which desire constitutes our will tends to matter to us. In cases of conflict, we care about which first-order desire wins out. So it's not just that I want to have the desire to exercise more, but it's that I want my desire to exercise more to be effective in moving me to action. I want it to be my will. When someone has this kind of second-order desire, when she wants a certain desire to be her will, this is what Frankfurt calls a *second-order volition*. And it's the having of second-order volitions that Frankfurt takes to be essential to personhood.

Since the capacity for second-order volitions requires a certain amount of reflection, Frankfurt's account in this way seems to entail that any person will have self-consciousness. It also seems to entail that any person will have the capacity to reason. As Frankfurt says, "it is only in virtue of his rational capacities that a person is capable of becoming critically aware of his own will and of forming volitions of the second order. The structure of a person's will presupposes, accordingly, that he is a rational being" (Frankfurt 1971, 11–12).

But, in contrast to accounts in the Lockean tradition, Frankfurt's account does not treat the capacities for self-consciousness and reason as either singly or jointly sufficient for personhood. To see this, we might consider an individual that Frankfurt calls a *wanton*, i.e., an individual who has first-order desires, and possibly even second-order desires, but no second-order volitions. A wanton has desires, and his desires move him to action, but he doesn't care about which of his desires move him to action. Though he may be self-conscious, and though he may deliberate about different courses of action, his actions will ultimately be determined by his strongest desires and, more importantly, the wanton does not care which of his desires is the strongest.

As we have seen, Frankfurt treats the capacity for second-order volition as necessary for personhood. But there is another, closely related capacity that he also thinks is necessary for personhood:

> It is only because a person has volitions of the seco
> that he is capable both of enjoying and of lacking fr   f
> the will. The concept of a person is not only, then, t   t
> of a type of entity that has both first-order desires   li-
> tions of the second order. It can also be construed as the
> concept of a type of entity for whom the freedom of its will
> may be a problem. (Frankfurt 1971, 14)

A person enjoys freedom of the will when she has the will that she wants to have, i.e., when the desire that moves her to action is the desire that she wants to be her will. Not all persons actually have free will – often the desire that moves us to action is not the one that we want to be acting on – but what makes us persons is in part the fact that freedom of the will is a possibility for us. For wantons, in contrast, it is not. Since wantons do not have second-order volitions, there can be no question of whether they have the will they want to have. There is no sense in which they want their will to be one way or another.

I won't here attempt to adjudicate between Frankfurt's account and accounts in the Lockean vein. But, before closing, it will be useful to return to our list above of candidates for metaphysical personhood and review how some of these candidates fare on the two different accounts. In particular, it will be useful to make two points. First, it should be clear that both accounts suggest that at least some humans are not persons in the metaphysical sense. Newborn infants lack many of the traits required by accounts in the Lockean vein, and even young children will lack the capacity for second-order volition. Individuals in persistent vegetative states who have lost all higher brain function will not count as persons. As for individuals with severe cognitive impairments, more would need to be known about the extent of those impairments. Second, it should be clear that both accounts leave open the possibility that at least some non-humans are persons. In this section, I have occasionally called upon examples from science fiction to help make this point. But as compelling as such examples are, it can also be useful to have some real-world examples before us. I'll do this in the next section, when we turn to consider in more detail animals often mentioned as candidates for personhood: dolphins and the great apes.

1.3   Case Studies: Dolphins and the Great Apes

As more and more has been learned about various animal species, many of them have been revealed to have incredibly sophisticated abilities. Researchers working with corvids – a group of birds that includes crows, magpies, and ravens – claim that the birds show evidence of being able to understand what other birds are thinking. After working with parrots for over three decades, the researcher Irene Pepperberg claims that their intricate vocabulary is not simply a function of mimicry; rather, parrots can understand the words they use, engage in abstract thinking, and can understand complex relations. For example, experiments have suggested that parrots can conceptualize notions of color, sameness and difference, and quantity.

In discussions of personhood, however, the two types of animals most often discussed are dolphins and the great apes – a group that includes gorillas, chimpanzees, bonobos, and orangutans. (Interestingly, the word "orangutan" is a contraction of two Malay words that mean "person of the woods.") As we will see, evidence suggests that members of these species have many of the capacities that are usually deemed to be central to metaphysical personhood.

To start, let us return to John Locke's influential definition of personhood: a person is a being who can consider itself as itself. How might we test for the capacity for self-awareness? During a brief conversation, a robotic telemarketer may convey an impression of self-awareness and even go so far as to deny being a robot. When confronted with such cases, however, we tend to deny that the robotic telemarketer is genuinely self-aware. Rather, it is simply doing a convincing imitation of genuine self-awareness. Any test for self-awareness, then, needs to be able to distinguish the mere appearance of self-awareness from the real thing.

In 1970, psychologist Gordon Gallup Jr. developed the mirror self-recognition test – often simply called the mirror test – to determine whether non-human animals had a sense of self. First, over a period of several days, a group of chimpanzees were exposed to a mirror. Next, several of them were placed under anesthesia during which time researchers applied some harmless red dye to their foreheads. Once the dye dried, it had no smell and could not be felt, so the chimps had no way of knowing that they had been marked. Upon waking, when these marked chimpanzees saw themselves in the mirror, they reacted noticeably to the mark on their foreheads. Such a chimpanzee might touch its own forehead, examine its fingers afterwards, angle itself so as to have a better view, and so on. In short, the behavior showed that the chimpanzee could tell that it was seeing itself in the mirror rather than another chimpanzee (Gallup 1970). Since it doesn't seem that one could recognize oneself in a mirror unless one had a sense of self, the mirror test is thought to demonstrate self-awareness.

As a point of comparison, it's useful to note that human infants and toddlers routinely fail versions of the mirror test. When very young children see themselves in a mirror, they take themselves to be seeing another child. Only at the age of approximately 18–24 months does a child become capable of recognizing the image in the mirror as herself.

Following Gallup's work with chimpanzees, other great apes such as bonobos and orangutans have also passed the mirror test. Interestingly, when six gorillas were tested, none of them passed. Though this was initially taken as evidence for the claim that gorillas lacked the capacity for self-awareness, researchers have subsequently questioned this conclusion, citing gorillas' natural aversion to making eye contact with one another as an alternate explanation. Moreover, researchers working with Koko the gorilla claim that she has passed a version of the mirror test, modified in such a way that she would not have to be anesthetized:

> During a series of ten-minute sessions videotaped over a three-day period, Koko's brow was wiped with a warm, damp, pink washcloth. During one of these sessions, the washcloth had been dipped in clown paint of the same pink color. In the sessions in which she was unmarked, Koko touched the target area an average of only one time per session. During the fifth session when her brow was marked, she touched the target area forty-seven times, only after viewing it in the mirror.... It is evident that Koko recognised the altered image as her own. (Patterson and Gordon 1993, 71)

Though many species have repeatedly failed the mirror test, it is not only primates who have passed. Despite having brains that are strikingly different from those of primates in many respects, dolphins have also shown evidence of self-recognition via a version of the mirror test. Working with two captive dolphins at the New York State Aquarium, researchers Diana Reiss and Lori Marino found clear evidence that the dolphins could recognize themselves in a mirror. For example, when marked under the chin, the dolphin would repeatedly exhibit upward neck stretches when near a reflective surface; when marked behind the left pectoral fin, the dolphin would exhibit sustained left-side orientation. Reiss and Marino take their studies to "provide definitive evidence that the two dolphins in this study used the mirror (and other reflective surfaces) to investigate parts of their bodies that were marked" (Reiss and Marino 2001, 5942).

Further evidence that dolphins are capable of self-awareness relates to their use of a "signature whistle." A signature whistle, developed as early as one month of age, functions similarly to the way a name functions for a human. A dolphin uses it to broadcast information about its identity to other nearby dolphins and also to make contact with them. Dolphins also seem to use their whistles to locate one another. For example, they may be used by a mother and her calves who become separated. Dolphins also sometimes emit the signature whistles of other dolphins, suggesting that they are trying to get that dolphin's attention. A dolphin's signature whistle stays the same over the course of its life.

In addition to serving as evidence for dolphins' capacity for self-awareness, the use of signature whistles serves as evidence of dolphins' capacity for communication. Since the late 1960s when a chimpanzee named Washoe was taught American Sign Language, various methods have been employed in an attempt to communicate with great apes. In addition to sign language, researchers have used systems involving plastic tokens and keyboards. But since dolphins don't have hands, they cannot be taught sign language, and the other communication systems used with the great apes are not easily adaptable to an aquatic form of life. The scientific evidence to date thus focuses primarily on dolphins' ability for language comprehension rather than on their ability to communicate with us.

Perhaps the most extensive dolphin communication studies have been conducted by Louis Herman, a professor at the University of Hawaii. Working with two bottlenose dolphins named Phoenix and Akeakamai, Herman has shown that dolphins have impressive comprehension abilities. Each dolphin was taught a different communication system. While Phoenix was taught an acoustic language consisting of computer-generated whistles, Akeakamai was taught a gestural language consisting of hand signals. Each dolphin was able to follow complex commands involving objects (hoop, pipe, ball, etc.), actions (fetch, toss, go through), and directions (left/ right, surface/bottom). To give just one example, Phoenix could differentiate between an instruction that required her to go to the hoop at the surface and take it to the basket at the bottom, and an instruction that required her to go to the basket at the bottom and take it to the hoop at the surface. By using paddles that were placed in the pool, the dolphins were also able to answer yes/no questions. Importantly, the two dolphins' performance was significantly better than chance. Over the course of the studies, the two dolphins followed instructions correctly more than 80% percent of the time.

What about other features that have been invoked in discussions of metaphysical personhood? There seems to be no doubt that great apes and dolphins are capable of pleasure and pain, and they also seem capable of experiencing emotion. Dolphins have been known to exhibit both fear and grief. When a tankmate dies, for example, a dolphin in captivity may refuse food. Similarly, Koko the gorilla exhibited signs of grief when a beloved kitten died. Moreover, her sign language vocabulary includes many words for emotions ("happy," "sad," "afraid," etc.) that she seems to use appropriately. Though it's not clear how we could develop a scientific measure of the kind of autonomy that Frankfurt sees as central to personhood, it's worth noting that dolphins and great apes both seem to make deliberate behavioral choices. They can, for example, delay gratification until a later time.

As the discussion of this section shows, then, the kinds of features that seem central to metaphysical personhood do not seem to be unique to humans alone. Depending on our precise definition of metaphysical personhood, it seems plausible that both dolphins and the great apes at least come very close. Insofar as we find this conclusion difficult to accept, it seems likely that we're guilty of some kind of humancentric bias.

In fact, a humancentric bias may well creep into the very specification of our account of metaphysical personhood in the first place. Given that humans are our paradigm example of metaphysical persons, we tend to look at humans when drawing up a plausible list of necessary and sufficient conditions. No matter how careful we try to be when constructing such a list, biases – often implicit – crop up in unexpected ways. We recognize the problematic aspect of including features such as "is a biped" or "has opposable thumbs" on the list. But features that appear unproblematic on the surface may nonetheless reflect humancentric assumptions. To give just one example, consider intelligence. On the face of it, a requirement in terms of intelligence may seem to be species-neutral. But how do we define intelligence? As persuasively argued by Thomas White, an American philosopher who has written extensively about dolphins, intelligence in dolphins may look quite different from intelligence in humans; after all, there are very different challenges to be met navigating life in the water compared to navigating life on land. Moreover, an aquatic environment provides different means for solving problems from those provided by a land environment. We use our hands to solve all sorts of problems – and there may be reason to think the co-evolution of the human brain and the human hand has been a significant force in shaping human intelligence. But of course, dolphins don't have hands.

Douglas Adams pokes fun at our humancentric bias in his novel, *The Hitchhiker's Guide to the Galaxy*:

> For instance, on the planet Earth, man had always assumed that he was more intelligent than dolphins because he had achieved so much – the wheel, New York, wars and so on – whilst all the dolphins had ever done was muck about in the water having a good time. But conversely, the dolphins had always believed that they were far more intelligent than man – for precisely the same reasons. (Adams 1979, 156)

More seriously, the worry about humancentricity is nicely exemplified by some remarks made by dolphin researcher Herman in an interview with *Omni* magazine (Kaplan 1989). In defending his claims about the linguistic abilities of Phoenix and Akeakamai, Herman noted that it would be "unduly restrictive" to require an animal be able to do all the things a human can do before we say that it has the capacity for language. From the perspective of a dolphin, for example, it might naturally look like humans lack swimming ability. We can't leap 15 feet above the surface, or stay underwater for 15 minutes, or swim at a speed of over 25 kilometers per hour. As we continue our investigation into persons and personal identity in the rest of this book, we will thus need to be careful to guard against a humancentric bias.

Further Reading

When undertaking an exploration into personhood, John Locke (1689/1975) is an excellent place to begin. Tur (1987) provides a useful introduction to legal personhood. Frankfurt's view of metaphysical personhood is developed in Frankfurt (1971). Rorty's (1976) anthology, *The Identities of Persons*, contains several useful papers on this topic. Warren (1997) surveys a variety of accounts of moral personhood. For discussion of mental capacity accounts in particular, useful sources include Tooley (1983) and Regan (2004). An important critique is offered in Kittay (2005). The account developed in Dennett (1976) has proved influential in subsequent discussions of both moral and metaphysical personhood. Likewise, the discussion in Feinberg and Levenbook (1992), which has the virtue of being particularly accessible, is also relevant to both moral and metaphysical personhood. For a criticism of the coherence and usefulness of the notion of personhood, see Beauchamp (1999).

Many of the articles in Cavalieri and Singer (1993) take up issues of personhood relating to gorillas and other apes. Considerable information about Koko is available online at www.koko.org and also in Patterson and Gordon (1993). For an academic discussion of Alex the parrot, see Pepperberg (2002); for a more popularized account, see Pepperberg (2008). A short and accessible introduction to the personhood of dolphins can be found in White (2010); for more comprehensive discussions, see White (2007) and Herzing and White (1998).

There are many works of fiction and film relevant to personhood. I recommend especially the novella *Bicentennial Man* by Isaac Asimov and the 1982 film *Blade Runner* directed by Ridley Scott. (Note that the director's cut version is better than the original release.)

2
The Psychological Approach to Personal Identity

In the previous chapter, we dealt with the identification question: what properties must a being have to count as a person? In this chapter we begin to consider the reidentification question: What makes a person the same person over time? Both of these questions concern personal identity. But while the identification question is a *synchronic* question – a question concerning personal identity *at a time* – the reidentification question is a *diachronic* question – a question concerning personal identity *over time*.

Suppose you buy a six-pack of Coke. There's a sense in which the cans are identical to one another – namely, that each can looks exactly like the others. But there's also a sense in which the cans are not identical to one another – namely, that there are six different cans. The sense in which the cans are identical is typically referred to as *qualitative identity*; the cans share all their qualities in common. The sense in which the cans are not identical is typically referred to as *numerical identity*; they are not one and the same thing but rather six things. Likewise, identical twins are qualitatively identical but numerically distinct. In this chapter, in investigating the question of personal identity, the kind of identity or sameness that is relevant is numerical identity. Is this tired-looking woman I've just bumped into in the Dallas airport the very same person as the energetic young girl who was my bunkmate at summer camp? Is the individual I now see on the sidewalk ahead of me the same person as the individual who cut in front of me in line at the supermarket last week?

The distinction between qualitative and numerical identity does not exhaust the senses of identity in play in ordinary discussion of personal identity. Sometimes when we talk about someone's identity we are picking out the role that they play in a particular situation. In one context someone might be a philosophy professor, in another context a soccer mom, and in yet another context a volunteer firefighter. Sometimes when we talk about someone's identity we mean to be referring to how they would identify themselves, or how they think of themselves "first and foremost." Here there are many possible candidate identities – one might think of oneself as a Democrat, as a Christian, as a veteran, as a lesbian, as a Latina, and so on. Identity in this sense is what makes someone who they really are. We will turn to these sorts of issues about personal identity in chapter 5 when we turn to the characterization question.

As we noted in chapter 1, our inquiry into persons and personal identity in this book is a metaphysical one. The question of reidentification that we are interested in is thus a question about *what makes it the case* that someone is the same person over time, not a question about *how we can tell* that someone is the same person over time. Suppose I had a childhood friend with an extremely distinctive laugh. Decades later, at my twenty-fifth high school reunion, someone unfamiliar-looking greets me by name. As she realizes that I don't recognize her, she starts laughing. And then, all of a sudden, I know exactly who she is. The way that I reidentified my childhood friend was by her laugh; that's how I could tell who she was. But though her laugh provided me with an _epistemological criterion_ for personal identity over time, it was not a _metaphysical criterion_. Her laugh is not what makes her the same person over time. Even were she to lose her laugh due to a vocal chord injury, she would still be numerically the same person. Although sometimes our epistemological means of reidentification will be related to the metaphysical facts, these two different criteria might well be distinct.

Metaphysical questions of reidentification are not unique to persons. We might wonder, for example, what makes something the same table over time, or what makes something the same car over time, and so on. These questions have particular force when the entity in question undergoes dramatic qualitative change, as when a table is repainted or when a car gets an entirely new engine. One compelling example that is often invoked in discussions of object identity over time concerns the Ship of Theseus, a sailing vessel made entirely of wood. After some time on the seas, one of the ship's boards rots and is replaced. Clearly the replacement of a single board does not affect the identity of the ship. But over a period of time, as the ship is regularly in use, other boards begin gradually to rot as well, and they are each replaced one by one. Eventually, each board of the ship has been replaced by an entirely new one. None of the original matter of the ship remains. So is the ship we ended up with the same ship – that is, numerically the same ship – as the one that we started with?

This puzzle case was first introduced into discussion in the first century by the Greek historian Plutarch, but an important twist was later added in the seventeenth century by English philosopher Thomas Hobbes. Suppose that each time we remove a rotting board, we place it in a storage shed. And suppose also that, once all of the original boards have been removed and stored in the shed, we reassemble them in the same configuration as had been previously used. We now have two ships: one that has been regularly and continually in use, and one that appears to have just come into existence but that contains all the original matter from the ship that had first set sail. So which one is the Ship of Theseus?

issue of the Ship

As we consider the reidentification question over the next three chapters, we will encounter similar sorts of puzzles that arise with respect to persons. Some of these puzzling cases – such as situations involving amnesia and dissociative identity disorder – are drawn from real life. Others – be they *Freaky Friday*-like scenarios in which two bodies seem to swap minds or upload scenarios in which a mind is transferred from body to machine – are, at least at present, purely hypothetical. As we will see, sorting out what is required for the continued existence of a person is a difficult task.

Freaky Friday

2.1 Locke's Memory Theory

Just as contemporary discussions of personhood have been greatly influenced by the work of seventeenth-century English philosopher John Locke, so too have contemporary discussions of personal identity over time. In fact, Locke is often credited with originating the philosophical discussion about personal identity. He was really the first philosopher to give attention to the subject in its own right.

As we saw in chapter 1, Locke considers personhood to consist in the capacities for reason and reflection. On his view, a person is a thinking, intelligent being who can "consider it self as it self" (Locke 1689/1975, 335). This account of personhood leads naturally to an account of personal identity over time:

> since consciousness always accompanies thinking, and 'tis that, that makes every one to be, what he calls *self*; and thereby distinguishes himself from all other thinking things, in this alone consists *personal Identity*, i.e. the sameness of a rational Being: And as far as this consciousness can be extended backwards to any past Action or Thought, so far reaches the Identity of that *Person*; it is the same *self* now it was then; and 'tis by the same *self* with this present one that now reflects on it, that that Action was done. (1689/1975, 335)

To extend one's consciousness backwards is to remember; thus Locke's theory is often referred to as *the memory theory*. For Locke, personal identity consists in connections of memory.

Of course, memory comes in many different forms. Particularly relevant here is the distinction between *factual* and *experiential* memory. I have all kinds of factual memories – I remember that California was granted statehood in 1850, that Boardwalk is the highest-valued property in Monopoly, that Germany won the 2014 World Cup, and so on. Some of my factual memories are directly correlated with experiential memories: Not only do I remember that Germany won, but I remember watching the victory on television. My other factual memories might not be correlated with any experiential memories. For example, I wasn't alive when California achieved statehood and I don't even recall learning this fact. Experience memories are essentially first-personal, that is, they are remembered from the first-person perspective. Importantly, this is not to say that I can't have experiential memories involving other people. My memory of watching the final match of the 2014 World Cup, for example, includes my older son, who was sitting next to me on the sofa as we watched. But my memory of the experience is from my perspective, not his. I cannot *remember* watching the World Cup from my son's perspective because I did not experience it from his perspective in the first place.

When Locke accounts for personal identity in terms of memory, he has experiential memory in mind. To make this more explicit, we might specify his theory as follows:

> **Locke's memory theory**: A at time t1 is identical to B at some later time t2 if and only if B remembers an experience had by A.

In offering his memory theory, Locke is reacting at least in part against previous writers who defined personal identity in terms of the soul. On Plato's view, for example, each individual is composed of two parts: a body and a soul. While the body is mortal, the soul is not. A soul that's joined with a particular body existed before the body came into existence and will continue to exist after the body goes out of existence. Plato does not think that the soul carries any experiential memories with it. Were a particular soul that had previously been joined with one body now to join with a new body, it would not bring along with it any memories from its previous embodiment. It's for this reason, says Locke, that personal identity cannot consist in sameness of soul. As this suggests, his criticism does not depend on the assumption that souls do not exist. Even if there are such things as souls, our possession of a soul is not what makes us the same person over time.

To develop this criticism of the soul theory and to help motivate his own view, Locke proposes a thought experiment using figures from Greek mythology such as Nestor and Thersites. According to legend, both of these men were Greek soldiers who were present at the siege of Troy. Now suppose that immortal souls exist, and that you happen to have the soul of one of these men. Does that make you identical with him? Locke thinks the supposition is absurd. For example, as depicted by Homer in the *Iliad*, Thersites was struck across the back and shoulders by Odysseus in response to his having sharply criticized Agamemnon; after being hit, he sat cowering, crying, and in pain. But presumably you don't have any memory of that experience and even now, upon hearing the story, you presumably don't feel that you were once beaten by Odysseus. On Locke's view, having the same soul as Thersites is as incidental to your personal identity as if your body happened to be made up of some of the same particles of matter that once constituted Thersites' body. As he argues: "the same immaterial Substance without the same consciousness, no more [makes] the same Person, by being united to any Body, than the same Particle of matter without consciousness united to any Body, makes the same Person" (Locke 1689/1975, 339–40). Were one to find oneself with experiential memories of Thersites' actions, however, then matters would be different. To have experiential memories of Thersites' actions is to be one and the same as Thersites.

2.2   Senility and Sleep

Though there's something intuitively appealing about Locke's account of personal identity, there also appear to be some fairly obvious problems with it. One such problem was first raised by the Scottish philosopher Thomas Reid, a contemporary of Locke's. Reid (1785) presents us with the following case: consider a brave officer who achieves an important military victory. At the time of the victory, the officer remembers that as a young boy he once stole some apples from a neighboring orchard. Now consider the officer many years later. Having retired from the military at the rank of general, he has become senile. Though he remembers the glory of his military victories, he has forgotten the indiscretions of his youth and has no memory of having stolen his neighbor's apples.

Since the retired general remembers the brave officer's victory, Locke's theory treats them as one and the same person. Likewise, since the brave officer remembers the naughty boy's theft, Locke's theory treats him them as one and the same person. But since the retired general does not remember the naughty boy's theft, Locke's theory does not treat them as one and the same person. Unfortunately, this means that Locke's theory commits him to a violation of the principle of the transitivity of identity. According to this ← *issue* principle, if *a* is identical to *b*, and *b* is identical to *c*, then *a* *for* is identical to *c*. So if the senile general is identical to the *Locke* brave officer, and the brave officer is identical to the naughty boy, then it should follow that the senile general is identical to the naughty boy. But, as we've seen, this is something that Locke has to deny.

Our intuitions often pull us in different directions, so it would be rare for a philosophical theory to be able to accommodate all of our intuitive judgments. One usually has to bite some bullet or other. To violate the transitivity of identity, however, is to reject not just an intuition but a core logical principle. The problem raised by Reid's brave officer case is thus a very serious one. Moreover, the brave officer case is not an isolated example. Things happen to us that we remember distinctly for a while, and then such memories fade from view. At 20 years of age, you might distinctly remember your 16th birthday, but not your 12th birthday – even though you distinctly remembered your 12th birthday when you turned 16.

Fortunately, there is a simple modification that can be made to Locke's theory to account for this kind of case and thereby avoid violating the principle of the transitivity of identity. As stated, Locke's theory requires there to be a direct memory connection between two persons in order for them to be the same person. But, still in keeping with the general spirit of the theory, we can focus on *continuity of memory* instead. Consider a long braided rope. There might be no single strand of fiber running from beginning to end. But there are overlapping strands throughout the entire rope, so that even when there is no direct strand between two points, there will be strands from each of those points to other points such that we can trace a continuous path of fibers for the entire length of the rope. We might think of the memories of a person forming a similar kind of braid. Though there is no 'strand' of memory directly connecting the senile general to the naughty boy, both of these stages are connected by memory strands to the brave officer, and so they both form a part of the same braid of memories.

This gives us the following modification to Locke's theory:

> *The modified memory theory*: A at time t1 is identical to B at some later time t2 if and only if there is continuity of experience memory between B and A.

Given that this modification allows a memory theorist to avoid the problem raised by Reid, we seem to have a significant improvement over Locke's original account. Unfortunately, however, another problem immediately arises: there seem to be segments of an individual's life that are entirely disconnected from the braid of memories. In fact, such segments seem to occur each night during periods of dreamless sleep. During that time, an individual has no experience memories of what she's done while awake, nor does she later remember anything from that time. So there is no continuity of memory between periods of dreamless sleep and other times of her life. But surely Jane asleep is the same person as Jane awake.

We might worry about other possible disconnected periods as well. Sometimes a person is briefly knocked unconscious, for example. Sometimes people have temporary bouts of amnesia. Sometimes a person might go into a deep meditative trance where she completely empties her mind. When someone effusively proclaims how meditation has changed her life, however, she probably doesn't mean to say that she becomes a numerically different person during her meditative states.

Faced with such problems, we might wonder whether we should abandon the memory account. Before giving up hope, however, it seems worth considering another possible modification that again seems to be within the general spirit of what Locke had in mind. This modification relies crucially on a distinction between *occurrent* and *non-occurrent* mental states. Right now you have all sorts of beliefs that are not present to your mind. Consider your belief that earth is a planet. Now that you've read the previous sentence, this belief is present to your mind. But before reading that sentence, it (presumably) wasn't. Beliefs that are present to the mind are what philosophers call *occurrent beliefs*. Beliefs that are not present to the mind are non-occurrent beliefs. Memories too can be either occurrent or non-occurrent. Much as he might dwell on his former glory, the retired general presumably doesn't have his memory of his brave deeds as an officer before his mind during his every waking moment. Sometimes those memories are non-occurrent.

So now let's conduct a very simple experiment. Recall some proud achievement from your past and bring your experience memory of it to mind. Prior to complying with my instruction, your memory of the achievement was not before your mind; now it is. But even prior to complying with my instruction, it seems clear that you were the same person as the person who accomplished that achievement. So memories do not need to be present before your mind to belong to a continuity chain of memories – rather, what seems to matter is that they could be brought before your mind if you tried. This suggests that we should further modify the modified memory theory:

> **The re-modified memory theory**: A at time t1 is identical to B at some later time t2 if and only if there is continuity of memory between B and A, where continuity of memory does not require that memories are actually occurrent but only that they be potentially occurrent.

This modification seems to be able to handle nicely the problem of dreamless sleep. While in a dreamless sleep, though you don't have any occurrent memories, you have all sorts of potentially occurrent memories. It also seems to handle the problem of meditative trances. But what about cases where someone is briefly knocked unconscious? Here matters start to get slightly trickier. Do we really want to claim that memories are potentially available to the unconscious individual?

The trickiness here can be made more vivid by considering longer cases of unconsciousness. When someone has been in a coma for weeks, months, even years, it seems slightly more troubling to say that the memories are potentially available to her. On the one hand, it's tempting to insist that they are potentially available to her. If she weren't in a coma, she could call those memories to mind. But, on the other hand, this leads us down a troubling slippery slope. For we could also say something similar about a corpse: after all, if she weren't dead, then she would be able to call those memories to mind. And perhaps even worse, the memories might be said to be potentially available to another individual entirely: after all, if she had been the one to have those experiences, then she would be able to call those memories to mind too.

The problem is that we need some principled way of distinguishing when memories are potentially occurrent from when they are not. Unfortunately, it turns out to be remarkably hard to draw this distinction, and it is not clear that it can adequately be done. This problem also relates closely to another problem, one that arises from an attempt to pin down what counts as a genuine memory. Exploring these issues – which are often referred to as *the problem of circularity* – will be the task of the next section.

2.3   The Problem of Circularity

Suppose someone didn't know what an umiak is, and I offered them the following definition: "an umiak is an umiak." Although I have said something true, the definition I've offered doesn't reveal anything about what an umiak is and is thus entirely unhelpful. In order for my definition to be at all illuminating, I would have to explain the notion of an umiak in terms of other notions, preferably familar ones. So I might say something like, "An umiak is a boat similar in construction to a kayak but significantly larger."

The unhelpfulness of my original definition can be explained by the fact that it is circular, i.e., the same term appears on both sides of the definition. But a definition might be circular even if the same word does not occur on both sides. Consider the following definition of "language" from Dictionary.com: "a body of words and the systems for their use common to a people who are of the same community or

nation, the same geographical area, or the same cultural tradition." Though the definition does not appear to be circular,
when we then look at the definition of "word" we find: "a
unit of language, consisting of one or more spoken sounds
or their written representation, that functions as a principal
carrier of meaning." Thus, the notion of *language* is defined
in terms of the notion of *word*, which is itself defined in terms
of the notion of *language*. In such a case, the circularity is
hidden beneath the surface. When the charge of circularity is
levied against the memory theory, it is a circularity of this
latter sort. On the surface, defining personal identity in terms
of continuity of memory does not seem to involve a circle.
But, as initially noted by Joseph Butler, an eighteenth-century
English bishop and philosopher, a proper understanding of
the notion of memory seems to presuppose the notion of
personal identity (Butler 1736). Thus, we have a circle – albeit
a hidden one.

Why might one think that memory presupposes personal
identity? To see this, let's consider two teenagers, Stella and
Bella, both of whom are big Beyoncé fans. Last night, Stella
went to a Beyoncé concert, had a great time, and now cher-
ishes her memories of the experience. But tickets were really
expensive, and Bella couldn't afford one. Fortunately for
Bella, her uncle is a skilled hypnotist (and willing in this case
to work for free), and after reading detailed descriptions of
the concert on social media, he hypnotizes her so that she
now believes that she went to the concert too. It seems to her
exactly as if she'd been there. She can tell you how Beyoncé
looked from where she takes herself to have been sitting,
what songs were played, how she felt when she danced along
to "Single Ladies," and so on. Just like Stella, she takes herself
to have cherished memories of attending the concert.

From the internal perspective, Stella and Bella are very
similar. Both of them take themselves to have experienced
the concert and to now remember having done so. But while
it seems natural to treat Stella's memories as real, it also seems
natural to treat Bella's memories as fake. What Bella takes
to be memories are only *pseudo-memories*. Importantly,
though, her pseudo-memories might be every bit as vivid and
detailed as Stella's. To explain why Bella's pseudo-memories
are merely apparent, then, it looks like we cannot rely on

anything about her mental state itself. Instead we have to rely on the fact that she wasn't actually at the concert. Since she didn't actually have the experience, any apparent memory of such an experience cannot be a real memory.

As this example makes clear, then, for something to count as a genuine memory of some event, that event must actually have been experienced by the person who seems to remember it. We can put this more formally as follows:

> *Memory*: A's apparent memory M of some event E is a genuine memory of E only if E was experienced by A.

But that means that the definition of memory presupposes the notion of same person: for some apparent memory of an experience to be a real memory of yours, you must have been the person to have experienced it.

Although philosophers love to invoke hypnotists, for those readers skeptical of such fanciful devices, the same point could have been made with more mundane examples. We often inadvertently appropriate the experiences of our friends, so much so that we believe them to have happened to us. Have you ever found yourself telling a story about some funny incident that you're sure once happened to you only to have your friend respond, "Hey that wasn't you. That was me!?" If it wasn't you who had the experience, then your apparent memory – no matter how deeply engrained and vivid – cannot be a genuine one. In this way, the notion of memory presupposes personal identity, and thus any definition of personal identity that relies on memory seems problematically circular.

To defend against the charge of circularity, a memory theorist has to find a way of defining memory that does not presuppose personal identity. Any such account would have to give us a way to distinguish real memories from merely apparent memories without invoking the notion of *same person*. Perhaps the most promising route to such a definition lies in causal accounts of memory. Causal theories are relatively common in philosophy. Perhaps the best-known causal theories around today are the causal theory of knowledge and the causal theory of reference. When I say, "Stephen is at soccer practice," what makes my use of the name "Stephen" refer to my son and not to Stephen Hawking or Stephen Colbert or some other Stephen? According to the causal theory of reference, my utterance of the name "Stephen" refers to my son because of a causal connection between it and him.

The causal theory of knowledge relies on a similar insight in explaining what counts as knowledge. Until the 1960s, many philosophers treated knowledge as equivalent to justified true belief, but an important paper by Edmund Gettier revealed this account to be lacking in certain ways. The problem arises from the fact that I might have a justified belief that happens to be true despite the fact that it is entirely unconnected from the truth. For example, suppose I turn on the television just in time to see Cuban baseball player Yoenis Céspedes being crowned the champion of the Homerun Derby. I then form the belief, "Céspedes won this year's Homerun Derby" – a belief that's plausibly justified by what I just saw on television. But though it's true that Céspedes is the victor of the 2014 Homerun Derby, it so happens that what was playing when I turned on the television was a replay of the 2013 Homerun Derby, an event that Céspedes also won. My belief, though both true and justified, is only accidentally so. It is not appropriately connected to the state of affairs in the world that makes it true. It thus doesn't seem that my belief rises to the level of knowledge. The causal theory of knowledge adds a further condition to rule out cases of accidental connection: knowledge requires a causal link, i.e., there must be a causal connection between someone's belief about an event and the event itself.

So now recall Stella and Bella. Both have apparent memories of having seen a Beyoncé concert but only Stella's is a real memory. Importantly, though, Stella's apparent memory was caused by the concert, while Bella's was caused by the hypnotist. If we require a causal link between a memory of an event and the event itself, it looks like we can explain the difference between Stella and Bella without having to invoke the notion of same person:

> *Causal theory of memory*: A's apparent memory M of some event E is a genuine memory of E only if M is causally connected to E.

Here we can see a direct parallel to the causal theory of knowledge: just as my belief about Céspedes cannot be knowledge because it is only accidentally connected to the fact in the world that it represents, Bella's apparent memory of the Beyoncé concert cannot be a real memory because it is only accidentally connected to the event in the world that it represents.

In this way, the causal account seems to offer us a solution to the problem of circularity. Unfortunately, however, matters are not quite this simple. Consider Ella, who also loves Beyoncé and who, like Stella, went to the concert. As the years go by, however, Ella has forgotten everything about it. This seems like such a shame, especially since she's still a huge fan of Beyoncé, so we take her to Bella's uncle, who does for Ella what he once did for Bella. Though Ella once had genuine memories of the concert, the apparent memories that she has right now are not themselves genuine; they've been implanted by a hypnotist. But the causal account does not give us the right result in this case. It's because Ella went to the concert that we took her to the hypnotist, and so there is a causal connection – albeit an indirect one – between the concert and the apparent memories. The causal theory thus has to accept Ella's memories as genuine.

Perhaps we can amend the causal theory of memory to accommodate this kind of case. Although there is a causal connection between Ella's memories of the concert and the concert itself, it doesn't seem to be a causal connection of the right sort. We can thus build a further requirement into the causal theory of memory:

> *Modified causal theory of memory*: A's apparent memory M of some event E is a genuine memory of E only if M is causally connected *in the right way* to E.

Importantly, for this account to be of use to the memory theorist, we would need a way to spell out the notion of "in the right way" without presupposing the notion of personal identity. Whether this can be done remains to be seen. (For one detailed attempt, see Perry 1975.)

Before closing this section, it will be useful to return briefly to the problem raised at the end of the previous section. As we saw, the memory theorist needs to provide an account of what it is for a memory to be potentially occurrent, i.e., the memory theorist needs to be able to distinguish between a sleeping individual (of whom we can truly say: were she to be woken, she could bring the memories before her mind) and a corpse (of whom we can truly say: were she to be alive, she could bring the memories before her mind). In essence, then, the memory theorist needs to explain when memories are potentially occurrent *in the right way*. Here too, any specification of what counts as "in the right way" will have to avoid presupposing the notion of personal identity.

2.4 The Psychological Theory

Despite the problems with the memory theory, memory does seem to play a key role in personal identity over time. But we might naturally think that memory doesn't tell the whole story. Consider Clive Wearing, a British musician who in 1985 contracted amnesia as a result of a serious brain infection. In addition to losing his ability to form new memories, Wearing also was afflicted by retrograde amnesia. As the neurologist Oliver Sacks describes it, Wearing suffered "a deletion of virtually his entire past" (Sacks 2007). But despite his amnesia, Wearing maintains many of his character traits – his musical ability, his elegant style, his fondness for dancing, and his deep and abiding love for his wife Deborah. Those who know him have no doubt that he's still Clive – a very changed Clive, no doubt, but still Clive. As this case suggests, it seems that a person can survive severe memory loss.

For this reason, we might naturally be led to think about other psychological connections that play a role in our personal identity over time. Last night before I went to bed, I formed the intention to exercise first thing this morning. When I woke up, I acted on this intention. While memories are backward-looking, connecting an individual to her past self, intentions are forward-looking, connecting an individual to her future self. Other connections run in both directions. The beliefs, desires, character traits, and habits that I have today connect both to the beliefs, desires, character traits, and habits of my past self and to those of my future self. Of course, I gain and lose beliefs and desires all the time, and my character traits and habits may also change over time, perhaps even dramatically so. But when there are overlapping chains of psychological connections over time – connections not just of memory, but also of intention, beliefs, desires, character traits, habits, and so on – we have psychological continuity. According to *the psychological theory* of personal identity, Locke's focus on memory was too narrow. Instead of trying to account for personal identity in terms of continuity of memory, such theorists instead account for personal identity in terms of continuity of psychology:

> *The psychological theory*: A at time t1 is identical to B at some later time t2 if and only if there is continuity of psychology between B and A.

In contemporary discussion of personal identity, the memory theory has largely been replaced by the psychological theory. Contemporary philosophers who have endorsed versions of this theory include Sydney Shoemaker, Derek Parfit, John Perry, and the late David Lewis, all of whom have made important contributions to its development. To avoid some of the problems facing the memory theory, psychological continuity is often explained in terms of *quasi-memory* rather than memory itself. According to Parfit (1984, 220), we can define quasi-memory as follows:

> *Quasi-memory*: A has a quasi-memory of some event E if (1) A seems to remember having experience E; (2) *someone* did have this experience; and (3) A's apparent memory is appropriately causally dependent on that past experience.

Quasi-memory is a wider concept than genuine memory. All genuine memories will be quasi-memories, but there may be quasi-memories that are not genuine memories. Unlike genuine memory, quasi-memory does not presuppose personal identity. By defining psychological continuity in terms of quasi-memory (and, analogously, other quasi-states), the psychological theorists can avoid problems of circularity.

There are two primary competitors to the psychological view. The first is the *physical theory*. While the psychological theory attempts to reduce personal identity to facts about continuity of psychological states, the physical theory attempts to reduce personal identity to facts about continuity of the body and/or biological continuity. As this suggests, despite the important differences between the psychological theory and the physical theory, they share a common commitment to reductionism; both theories are thus typically referred to as *reductionist* views. We will turn to a more complete discussion of the physical theory in chapter 4.

The second competitor to the psychological theory is the *further fact theory*. On this view, personal identity cannot be reduced to either psychological facts or physical facts. Rather, personal identity consists in some irreducible further fact. *[non reductional]* Someone who defines personal identity in terms of a soul, or a bare ego, offers this sort of view. Because this view denies the possibility of reduction, it is often referred to as a *nonreductionist* view.

Many of those who believe in the further fact view are motivated at least in part by considerations independent of personal identity. For example, religious commitments might give them independent reasons to believe in the existence of souls. But proponents of the view have also given philosophical justification for the existence of some such further fact. For example, let's return to the view of Bishop Butler, whose criticisms of Locke we encountered above. For Butler, we need to draw a distinction between two kinds of identity: identity in the loose and popular sense versus identity in the strict and philosophical sense. In the former sense of identity, we might say that an entity is the same even if its parts have undergone all sorts of change, but this will not be true in the latter sense of identity. In order to have identity in the strict sense, there must be something unchanging, i.e., there must be some further fact.

As we continue our discussion of the reidentification question, we will focus largely on the debate between the psychological theory and the physical theory, though we will briefly consider the further fact view in chapter 5. In the remainder of this chapter, however, we will first look in more detail at the psychological theory itself.

2.5   Transplants, Avatars, and Teleportation

Much of the motivation for the psychological theory stems from the consideration of puzzle cases. Normally, as we make our way through life, psychological continuity and physical continuity go hand in hand. My present self is both psychologically and physically continuous with my past 12-year-old self, and I assume the same goes for your present self and your past 12-year-old self. However, there are cases – both real and hypothetical – in which physical continuity and psychological continuity can be seen to come apart. According to advocates of the psychological approach, reflection on such cases shows us that psychological continuity is what matters for identity over time.

Let's first consider the case of brain transplantation. Imagine a possible future in which scientists have achieved the know-how and technology necessary for such a procedure to be successfully carried out. And let's also imagine a horrible car accident that leaves two individuals in critical condition. Brian, who was trapped in the car, has suffered severe burns over the majority of his body and his other organs are beginning to fail. Despite the fact that all of his brain functions remain intact, his death is imminent. Bodie, who was thrown from the car upon impact, suffered only minor bodily injuries. Unfortunately, however, he hit his head against a concrete pylon upon landing, and the force was so great that by the time the ambulance reaches the hospital he is declared brain-dead. Shortly thereafter, with the consent of both families, Brian's brain is transplanted into Bodie's body.

How should we imagine the case from here? When the individual with Bodie's body and Brian's brain – call him BB – wakes up after surgery, who has survived? Many people have the intuition that BB is the same person as Brian. If you yourself don't yet have clear intuitions about this case, it might help to consider it from the first-person perspective. If you were in Brian's position, if you had been in a terrible crash and your body was failing, would you opt to have your brain transplanted into a new body? And, more to the point, would you consider this a case in which you would survive? Will the person who wakes up after the surgery be you? Again, many people answer these questions in the affirmative.

So what do these intuitions show? Since BB has Brian's brain, it's natural to suppose that BB has Brian's psychology. He remembers (or, at least, he quasi-remembers) the crash from Brian's perspective, not Bodie's. More generally, he has Brian's personality traits. He thinks of Brian's family as his family. He mourns the loss of his friend Bodie, though he is grateful for the generosity of Bodie's family in allowing him to use Bodie's body. In fact, we might think the case has in some way been incorrectly described as a brain transplant. That description suggests, on analogy to heart transplants, that one person receives a new brain. But it's not really Bodie who gets a brain transplant; rather, it's Brian who gets a whole body transplant. And just as a successful heart transplant does not threaten one's identity, a successful whole body transplant does not threaten one's identity. This sort of case thus seems to support the psychological theory of personal identity, since the lack of bodily continuity does not seem to prevent BB from being Brian. Rather, it's the psychological continuity between BB and Brian that dictates that it's Brian rather than Bodie who has survived.

Of course, consideration of this case does not provide definitive support for the psychological theory. Some proponents of the physical theory do not share the intuition that they would survive such an operation, and they likewise insist that BB is identical to Bodie, not Brian. Such a view has been forcefully defended by the fictional character Gretchen Weirob in John Perry's *Dialogue on Personal Identity and Immortality* (1978). Facing near-certain death due to various bodily injuries she's sustained in a motorcycle accident, Weirob turns down the kind of procedure we have imagined. Though the survivor of the operation might *seem* to remember doing what she has done, and might even claim to be Gretchen Weirob, those facts are not enough to settle who the survivor is. As Gretchen says, that alone "does not make her me. For this could all be true of someone suffering a delusion, or a subject of hypnosis" (Perry 1978, 45). Other proponents of the physical theory admit that BB is identical to Brian but deny that this commits one to the psychological theory. On their view, what matters is not psychological continuity but continuity of the physical brain. Since BB has Brian's brain, BB is Brian. We will look at these sorts of responses when we look at the physical theory in more detail in chapter 4. In the meantime, however, it will be useful to consider some of the other cases often invoked to support the psychological theory.

The 2009 film *Avatar* directed by James Cameron takes place in the mid twenty-second century, at a time when Earth's natural resources have been severely depleted. The action occurs on Pandora, a planet whose atmosphere is toxic to humans and that is inhabited by a species of 10-foot-tall blue-skinned humanoids called the Na'vi. To make contact with the Na'vi and to gain their trust, the humans explore Pandora by way of the operation of what they call *avatars* – remote, artificial bodies that are human–Na'vi hybrids. The overall plot of the movie need not concern us here. For our purposes, what's most interesting is what happens at the end (and I apologize for the spoiler). One of the humans, Jake Sully, has his consciousness permanently transferred into his avatar body by a special Na'vi ritual and lives happily ever after among the Na'vi. This fictional case seems clearly to presuppose the psychological theory. Sully cannot live happily ever after among the Na'vi unless it's Sully who survives. Moreover, unlike in the transplant case considered above, here it's only the consciousness that's transferred, not the brain. Sully's original brain dies along with his original body. This further supports the claim made by psychological theorists about the previous case that what matters for survival is psychological continuity, not brain continuity.

Turning to one other case from science fiction, consider the transporter, a teleportation device used in the fictional world of *Star Trek*. As depicted by the shows and movies, the transporter is a form of near-instantaneous travel from one location to another – for example, from a spaceship orbiting a planet to the planet itself. Roughly speaking, the transporter scans an individual – Lieutenant Uhura, say – at the point of departure, records her "pattern," decomposes her, and then imposes that pattern on new matter at the point of arrival. Assuming the transporter works correctly, there seems to be no question that it's Uhura who has arrived at the appropriate coordinates. Though various Starfleet officers have their worries about using the transporter, their fear seems akin to the kinds of fear that people often have about air travel. The worry is that the device will fail, not that successful operation of the device amounts to death. Here then is another case in which psychological continuity seems to be prized over bodily or even brain continuity.

2.6 The Method of Thought Experiments

Psychological theorists have relied heavily on the sorts of puzzle cases that we've just considered in an effort to show their theory must be correct. Philosophers tend to refer to such cases as *thought experiments*. Unlike scientific experiments that are conducted in a physical laboratory, thought experiments are conducted in the laboratory of the mind, and the use of thought experiments is commonplace throughout philosophy – not just in metaphysics but also in epistemology, ethics, and every other area of philosophical inquiry. But, however common the method, it is often met with skepticism. In particular, when confronted with thought experiments that are purely science fiction, like the examples in the previous section, sometimes people are uncomfortable. Given that such examples are greatly removed from the world as we know it, one might naturally wonder what they could possibly show us about real life. The twentieth-century English philosopher Kathleen Wilkes has been particularly explicit in expressing this kind of concern: "Personal Identity has been the stamping-ground for bizarre, entertaining, and inconclusive thought experiments. To my mind, these alluring fictions have led discussion off on the wrong tracks; moreover, since they rely heavily on imagination and intuition, they lead to no solid or agreed conclusions, since intuitions vary and imaginations fail" (Wilkes 1988, vii). Importantly, psychological theorists are not the only ones invoking thought experiments. This method is commonplace in discussions of personal identity. But in the face of the kind of skepticism expressed by Wilkes, a response along the lines of "everyone is doing it" probably does not provide a compelling defense. Moreover, it is true that thought experiments play an especially crucial role in motivating the case for the psychological theory. Thus, it's worth considering what proponents of the theory might say in response to worries about this method.

Roughly speaking, psychological theorists seem to have three different possible answers available to them. First, they might rely on recent scientific developments that suggest that these cases are not as bizarre or far-fetched as they initially appear. Though such cases may at present be technologically out of reach, they are not – to use a term of Parfit's – "deeply impossible." For example:

- Scientists in the early 1980s successfully transplanted a piece of one mouse's brain into another's, and the recipient mouse survived in seven out of eight attempts. Moreover, human heart transplants have been successfully performed since the late 1960s, and doctors have also successfully transplanted kidneys, livers, lungs, pancreases, and small intestines, as well as eye tissue, bones, veins, and even faces. Such transplants typically involve donations from other humans but sometimes involve artificial organs. Patients who have received artificial hearts while waiting for donated hearts to become available have survived with such implanted devices for several years. Research continues into the development of artificial lungs, pancreases, and other organs. So, while it's true that, at the time that I'm writing, the idea of human brain transplants is still merely hypothetical, the possibility is not as remote as one might think.
- The inventor and futurist Ray Kurzweil, now director of engineering at Google, predicts that we will be able to upload the brain to a computer or android body via a straightforward scan-and-transfer procedure sometime in the late 2030s. In doing so, and thereby transcending the need for biological bodies, we will be able to achieve a kind of immortality. As he also explains, there are other emerging technologies that are even more powerful than scan-and-transfer brain uploading and that will soon enable us to make a gradual shift to a nonbiological form. First, in the 2020s, we will begin to augment our brains through the use of nanobots, so that some of our

cognition will be carried out by nonbiological means. The nonbiological portion of our cognitive architecture will begin to dominate by the 2030s, and it will continue to increase exponentially in capability. Then: "Although we are likely to retain the biological portion for a period of time, it will become of increasingly little consequence. So we will have effectively uploaded ourselves, albeit gradually, never quite noticing the transfer. There will be no 'old Ray' and 'new Ray,' just an increasingly capable Ray" (Kurzweil 2005, 202).

- In May 2014, a group of Dutch scientists succeeded in the "unconditional quantum teleportation" of data from one spot to another. As reported in the journal *Science*, experiments enabled the scientists to transfer information contained in one quantum bit to a different quantum bit located 3 meters away without the information having travelled through the intervening space. Though this is still a far cry from the teletransportation of objects, let alone human beings, it makes that possibility seem less remote.

This first response tries to deny that the examples used are mere science fiction. But psychological theorists also have available to them a different kind of response, one that accepts that such scenarios are unlikely to be realized any time soon (or perhaps ever). For, even if consciousness transfers and teleportation will never be actually achieved, the mere *possibility* of such scenarios is meant to be enough to show that the psychological theory is correct. Theories of personal identity are not just meant to be truths but are meant to be *necessary* truths. Consider other necessary truths, like the claim that four is an even number or that a circle has no corners. Since these are necessary truths, we cannot even coherently describe a situation in which four is an odd number or in which there is a cornered circle. Any such apparent descriptions wouldn't make sense. Likewise, if it were necessarily true that personal identity consists in physical continuity, we shouldn't be able to coherently describe a case in which A is the same person as B even though there is not physical continuity between them. Such a case should make as little sense as a case in which there was a cornered circle.

Since the scenarios above involving consciousness trans-fers and teleportation seem coherent when we explore them carefully via imagination, it looks like physical continuity theories must be false. And one could say something similar about the further fact view.

To my mind, these first two responses on behalf of the psychological theorist are pretty compelling. But, should there still be doubts, the psychological theorists might try a third kind of response. In particular, they may suggest that we can turn from science fiction and futuristic scenarios back to real life. In their view, there are real-life cases (or cases drawn very closely from real-life situations) that support their theory just as strongly as the science fiction cases already considered. We will consider some of these cases in detail in later chapters. For now, to give just one example, we might look to cases of dissociative identity disorder. In this condi-tion, which used to be called multiple personality disorder, an individual's identity has fragmented into what seem to be two or more distinct personalities. Given the vast differences among such personalities – from different likes and dislikes, to different genders, to different abilities – it has often been suggested that they are different persons. Insofar as this description of the phenomenon seems plausible, it reveals that we are thinking of a person's identity in psychological terms. One personality gets distinguished from another because there is significant lack of psychological continuity between them. We will return to a more complete discussion of dis-sociative identity disorder in chapter 4.

Further Reading

For a general discussion about the metaphysical issue of reidentification (including discussion of the Ship of Theseus case), see Chisholm (1977, ch. 3). Two excellent collections addressing the reidentification question with respect to persons are Perry (2008) and Martin and Barresi (2003); the papers in the first three sections of Perry (2008), including an excerpt from Locke (1689/1975), are particularly relevant to the memory theory. Perry (1978) provides a short and accessible introduction to the reidentification question via a dialogue format. Shoemaker (1984) and Parfit (1984, pt. 3) both provide influential defenses of the psychological theory.

In addition to Wilkes (1988), Gendler (2002) also provides a useful discussion of the role of thought experiments in discussions of personal identity.

For those interested in learning more about Ray Kurzweil, I recommend Barry Ptolemy's 2009 documentary *Transcendent Man*. Christopher Nolan's *Memento* (2000) and Michael Gondry's *Eternal Sunshine of the Spotless Mind* (2004) are two great films relevant to the role of memory in personal identity. *Total Recall*, a film based on the Philip K. Dick story "We Can Remember It For You Wholesale," provides a vivid example of the distinction between apparent memories and real memories. Personally, I'm partial to the original version from 1990 starring Arnold Schwarzenegger, but the 2012 remake is also good.

3

The Problem of Reduplication

As plausible as the psychological theory seems to be, various problems with it have been raised. In this chapter, we consider in detail one such problem: what's often referred to as *the problem of reduplication*. Historically, the problem seems to have initially been raised in the early eighteenth century by British philosopher Samuel Clarke in his correspondence with Anthony Collins, a wealthy English landowner. In Clarke's view, personal identity is to be explained by an immaterial soul. Collins, influenced by his friend Locke, was a defender of the memory theory. To explain Clarke's presentation of the problem fully would require us to delve too deeply into the details of the men's correspondence. But, roughly speaking, we can summarize Clarke's point this way: since it would be possible for God to resurrect many different individuals all of whom shared psychological continuity with some original person, personal identity must consist in something else that could not be duplicated in this fashion – namely, an immaterial soul. The problem also was raised by Thomas Reid in his criticisms of Locke. As he noted, "if the same consciousness can be transferred from one intelligent being to another... then two or twenty intelligent beings may be the same person" (Reid 1785, 114).

In the late 1950s, the reduplication problem was reintroduced to philosophical discussion through the work of English philosopher Bernard Williams, a critic of the psychological theory of personal identity. Williams asks us to consider the case of Charles, a man who one day suddenly wakes up with the memories and character of Guy Fawkes, a British mercenary who was part of a notorious plan to assassinate King James in the early seventeenth century. Though we might initially be skeptical of Charles' claims to be Fawkes, suppose that we eventually become convinced that he has indeed somehow been endowed with Fawkes' consciousness. Now suppose also that, some time later, the very same thing happens to Charles' brother Robert, i.e., he too wakes up with the memories and character of Guy Fawkes. If it could happen to Charles, why couldn't it also happen to Robert? And suppose too that Robert's claims to be Guy Fawkes are every bit as convincing as his brother's so that we eventually become convinced that he too has somehow been endowed with Fawkes' consciousness. In this case, then, we have two different men who are both psychologically continuous with Guy Fawkes. But, given that they are different men, not identical to one another, it does not seem that they can both be identical to Fawkes. Thus, concludes Williams, personal identity cannot consist solely in continuity of psychology.

Williams' case makes evident a basic problem for the psychological theory – namely, that psychological continuity can be reduplicated. But since his case does not specify a mechanism for the reduplication – it's due to unexplained magic that Charles and Robert wake up with Fawkes' psychology – it may not be wholly convincing. In the influential book *Reasons and Persons* (1984), however, English philosopher Derek Parfit provides us with just such a mechanism: teleportation. As a proponent of the psychological theory, Parfit himself believes that the reduplication problem can ultimately be resolved. But before we get to possible solutions, it will be helpful to have the problem laid out more clearly before us.

3.1   The Case of the Transporter Malfunction

Let's return once more to the transporter pad. As we imagined the workings of the transporter, the machine scans an individual at the point of departure, records her "pattern," dematerializes her, and then imposes that pattern on new matter at the point of arrival. But machines are finicky – both in real life and on *Star Trek* – and so it would be no surprise if the transporter were occasionally to malfunction. Of interest to us is a particular kind of malfunction. Suppose that, having recorded an individual's pattern and dematerialized her at the point of departure, the transporter imposes that pattern on two different bundles of matter at the point of arrival.

Let's make things more specific so that we can better consider this instance of reduplication. Margaret O'Malley, who lives in London, gets word that her sick father has taken a turn for the worse and that his death is now imminent. She needs to get to New York as quickly as possible so that she can see him before he dies. Price is no object, so she decides to travel by transporter rather than by plane. And she has safely travelled by transporter before. Last year she transported to Los Angeles and back when she needed to attend an important conference for work on short notice. At the transporter station in central London, she steps onto Pad 7. Her pattern is recorded, and she is dematerialized. Seconds later, two individuals simultaneously materialize into existence on the transporter pads at the downtown New York station. Both look exactly like Margaret, and both are psychologically continuous with Margaret. For example, each remembers (or at least quasi-remembers) stepping onto Pad 7, and each is anxious to get to the hospital to see Mr. O'Malley. To avoid prejudging the case, let's refer to the two individuals who materialize in New York as Meg and Peg (though they would each refer to themselves as Margaret). Clearly Meg is not numerically the same person as Peg. They are standing on different transporter pads, and one and the same person cannot be in two distinct places at once. Moreover, although each is psychologically continuous with Margaret, they do not share any direct psychological connections with one another. Neither can tell what the other is thinking. They also begin having different experiences as soon as they materialize – Meg experiences a doppelganger to her right, while Peg experiences a doppelganger to her left – and with each passing moment, their experiences continue to diverge. It might be slightly draftier where Meg is standing, for example, or the lights might be slightly brighter where Peg is standing. But though it's clear that Meg and Peg are numerically different persons from one another, their relationship to Margaret is harder to determine. Is either of them numerically the same person as Margaret? Are they both numerically the same person as Margaret? Or has Margaret tragically died as a result of the transporter malfunction?

Unfortunately for the psychological theorist, there seem to be no good answers to these questions. We have five options to consider:

1. Meg, not Peg, is identical to Margaret.
2. Peg, not Meg, is identical to Margaret.
3. Neither Meg nor Peg is identical to Margaret.
4. Both Meg and Peg are identical to Margaret.
5. There is no fact of the matter.

Both the first and second options seem problematic for the same reason: what basis could we possibly have for privileging one of these two individuals over the other? Whatever considerations count in favor of thinking that Meg is identical to Margaret also count in favor of thinking that Peg is identical to Margaret, and vice versa. Both are psychologically continuous with Margaret. Neither is bodily continuous with her. And since they materialized at the same time, neither has a head start over the other.

Option 3 might initially seem promising. When other kinds of entities split in two, they simply cease to exist. Consider the nation Czechoslovakia, which in 1993 split into the Czech Republic and Slovakia. Though both of these countries share much in common with the former Czechoslovakia, neither of them is identical to it. In 1993, the dissolution of Czechoslovakia meant that it ceased to exist. With this kind of case in mind, it seems plausible to think that the transporter malfunction similarly caused the "dissolution" of Margaret. When she splits into Meg and Peg, she ceases to exist. But now recall that this is not the first time that Margaret has used the transporter. She had previously transported to Los Angeles and back. Presumably, when you read the description of Margaret's situation above, you did not balk at this claim, i.e., you had no hesitation in accepting that an individual could survive travel by transporter. So now consider the person who stepped onto the transporter in London last year and the person who then stepped off the transporter in Los Angeles. We have no reason to doubt that they are the very same person, i.e., that both are Margaret. But the relationship between Margaret in London and Margaret in Los Angeles is exactly the same as the relationship between Margaret and Meg and it is also exactly the same as the relationship between Margaret and Peg. As this worry is often put: How can a double success be a failure?

Matters look no better for the fourth option. As we saw in the previous chapter, the principle of the transitivity of identity dictates that if **a** is identical to **b** and **b** is identical to **c**, then **a** must be identical to **c**. So if Meg is identical to Margaret and Margaret is identical to Peg, then Meg must be identical to Peg. But while much about the case under consideration is uncertain, one thing that seems entirely beyond question is that Meg is not identical to Peg. Thus, since option 4 entails the rejection of a core logical principle, it seems to be off the table.

Given the problems with the first four options, one might be tempted to think that the real problem with the case before us is that we are missing some critical information. If only we knew more, we could sort things out. But what more do we need to know? What facts are we missing? It's not clear that we could learn anything further that could help us to resolve matters. This sort of reasoning helps to motivate Option 5, which claims that there is simply no fact of the matter about Margaret's identity. Importantly, this is a metaphysical claim, not an epistemological one. To see what this amounts to, consider a situation in which we are trying to determine whether a given individual is tall. Some people are clearly tall, some people are clearly not, but there are also a bunch of borderline cases. Suppose that Omar is one of these cases. No amount of information could help us decide whether he is tall. Even if we establish Omar's precise height down to the millimeter, and we learn all the facts there were about the heights of other individuals, whether he is tall seems to be something about which there is no fact of the matter. Option 5 holds that the claim "Margaret is identical to Meg" is like the claim "Omar is tall." Just as it is indeterminate whether

Omar is tall, it is also indeterminate whether Margaret is identical to Meg.

With this clarified, option 5 seems rather unpalatable. How could there be borderline cases of identity? Though we might accept vagueness when it comes to predicates like "tall" and "bald," can we really accept that there is vagueness about our own numerical identity? As Parfit notes: "most of us are inclined to believe that, in any conceivable case, the question 'Am I about to die?' must have an answer. And we are inclined to believe that this answer must be either, and quite simply, Yes or No. Any future person must be either me, or someone else" (Parfit 1984, 214). As we will see in section 3.4 below, Parfit himself rejects this view. But I think he's right that most of us have such inclinations, and, more-over, that they're very strongly held. Suppose that, in advance of being transported, Margaret is informed that the trans-porters have been acting up lately and she is warned about the possibility of transporter malfunction resulting in redu-plication. Whether the transporter will malfunction during her teleportation is unknown. Because of this, there's uncer-tainty about her fate. But, according to option 5, even if we could definitively establish whether or not the transporter were going to malfunction, her fate would still be indetermi-nate. While trying to decide whether to go through with the transport, if she were to wonder, "If it does malfunction, does that mean that I'm going to die?", there would be no answer to her question. Likewise, even if both Meg and Peg get to the hospital in time to see Mr. O'Malley before he dies, there would be no answer to her question "Will I get to see my father one last time?"

As we have seen, then, none of the five options seems acceptable. The case of transporter malfunction thus presents a serious difficulty for the psychological theory. Of course, one might draw a different moral from this case. Rather than taking it to imply problems for the psychological theory, we might take it to show the implausibility of teleportation. Unfortunately, however, this response will not save the psy-chological theory, for the same problem could be raised without invoking transporters. First, we might consider *fission*. Though it seems implausible to imagine humans fis-sioning like amoebas, we can imagine an alien race of persons that has this capability. Such beings, we might suppose, do not procreate in the traditional sense. Instead, once every decade, they split into two. Each resultant being is psychologically continuous with the original, though, once split, the two beings have no direct psychological connections to one another. The possibility of such creatures raises the same difficulty raised by the case of transporter malfunction. Alternatively, we might consider *multiple upload*. As we saw in the last chapter, futurists like Raymond Kurzweil think that we will be able to upload our consciousness to computers by the middle of the twenty-first century. But, just as software can be installed on multiple devices, why couldn't our consciousness be installed on more than one device? As long as we countenance the possibility of the separation of psychological continuity from its physical instantiation, a possibility that seems central to the psychological theory, troublesome cases like these will arise.

Perhaps unsurprisingly, however, the psychological theorists deny that these problem cases force them to give up their theory. Roughly speaking, there have been three different kinds of responses attempted by such theorists, all three of which in some way attempt to rehabilitate option 3, i.e., the claim that neither Meg nor Peg is identical to Margaret:

- *The non-branching requirement.* Philosophers who take this line suggest that we need to modify the psychological theory to accommodate cases like that of transporter malfunction. In particular, rather than claiming that identity consists in psychological continuity, we should claim that identity consists in psychological continuity that takes a non-branching form. With this modification in place, it becomes apparent that Margaret is not identical to either of the individuals on the New York transporter pads.

  Ø·branch

- *Identity doesn't matter.* This response is typically conjoined with the non-branching requirement. Proponents of this response argue that, when thinking about what we care about with respect to our continued existence, we can come to see that identity is not what matters when we think about our futures. Even though neither Meg nor Peg is identical to Margaret (or, alternatively, even though there is no fact of the matter), what happens to Margaret is just about as good as ordinary survival.

- *Four-dimensionalism.* This way of rehabilitating option 3 involves the invocation of a metaphysical theory, *four-dimensionalism*, about the general nature of an object's persistence through time. In short, what we have failed to realize is that Meg and Peg both pre-existed the transporter malfunction. The individual we called "Margaret" really consisted of two persons all along.

In the remainder of this chapter, we take up each of these responses in more detail.

3.2 The Non-Branching Requirement

We might summarize the problem presented by cases of reduplication with the following argument:

1. Personal identity is a relation that holds one to one.
2. Psychological continuity is a relation that can hold one to many.
3. Thus, personal identity cannot consist in psychological continuity.

When we make a claim of identity, the identity sign is flanked by a single thing on each side (in fact, by the same thing on each side). It is logically impossible for one person to be identical to two or more distinct people. As we have already seen, identity is governed by transitivity: if **a** is identical to **b**, and **b** is identical to c, then **a** is identical to c. It is also reflexive (which means that everything stands in the identity relation to itself, i.e., **a** = **a**) and symmetric (which means that **a** is identical to **b** if and only if **b** is identical to **a**). Any relation governed by these principles is what's known as an *equivalence relation*, and any equivalence relation must hold only one to one. But, as shown by cases of transporter malfunction and multiple upload, the relationship of psychological continuity does not have this same structure. We might have one thing that is psychologically continuous with many other things. It thus does not look like psychological continuity is the right kind of relationship on which to base an account of personal identity.

According to some psychological theorists, however, this problem does not mean that we should abandon the psychological approach altogether. Rather, they suggest that we should instead focus on a slightly different relationship, namely, *non-branching psychological continuity*.

> *The non-branching psychological theory*: A at time t1 is identical to B at some later time t2 if and only if there is continuity of psychology between B and A, and there is no other person who stands in a relation of psychological continuity to A.

Returning to our options above, this theory commits itself to option 3. Neither Meg nor Peg is identical to Margaret. When we considered this option above, we worried that there seemed to be no principled way for the psychological theory to distinguish this instance of teleportation from Margaret's previous travels by teleportation. Consider the relationship of psychological continuity that held between Margaret prior to teleporting to Los Angeles and Margaret after, and now compare the relationship between Margaret and Meg (and also between Margaret and Peg). These relationships seem to be the same. But the non-branching psychological theory gives us a principled way to distinguish them. When Margaret traveled by transporter last year, since the teleportation resulted in only one person who was psychologically continuous with her, that person was identical to her. Now, when the transporter malfunctions, the fact that there are two people who stand in relations of psychological continuity to Margaret makes all the difference. Given that her psychological continuity has branched, neither Meg nor Peg is identical to her.

Insofar as it's reasonable to conclude that Margaret no longer exists after the transporter malfunction, the non-branching psychological theory seems to offer a reasonable solution to the problem of reduplication facing psychological theorists. Unfortunately, however, reflection on slightly different cases of reduplication makes reliance on the non-branching requirement seem considerably less plausible. Consider, for example, a case of delayed transporter malfunction. This time, the malfunction does not occur immediately, so after Margaret steps on the transporter pad in London, only one person – Meg, let's say – materializes in New York. According to the non-branching psychological theory, Margaret is identical to Meg. Five minutes later, however, Peg materializes in New York. Like Meg, Peg is also psychologically continuous with the pre-transport Margaret. At the point of Peg's materialization, then, Margaret's psychological continuity has branched. Thus, Meg is no longer identical to Margaret. As a result of Peg's arrival, Margaret has ceased to exist. Or consider a case of distant transporter malfunction. This time, only Meg materializes in New York. But, at the same time, Peg materializes on a transporter pad in New Zealand. From the perspective of Meg in New York, it seems as if the teleportation has been successful. From the perspective of Peg in New Zealand, it also seems that the teleportation was successful (though she's angry to have ended up halfway around the world from where she was supposed to). But both Meg and Peg are wrong. Since Margaret's psychological continuity has branched, she has now ceased to exist.

But surely these are very strange results! What has gone wrong? One way to diagnose the failure is in terms of a principle often referred to as the *only x and y* principle: whether some entity **x** is identical to some entity **y** must depend only on facts about **x** and **y**; it cannot depend on facts about other entities. This seems to be a plausible principle. How could the identity between Wonder Woman and Diana Prince, for example, depend on facts about Superman (or anyone else)? Unfortunately, however, the non-branching psychological theory is committed to a denial of this principle. On this view, whether Margaret is identical to Meg depends not only on facts about Margaret and Meg but also on facts about Peg. More generally, knowing that there is a relationship of psychological continuity between **x** and **y** is not enough to determine whether **x** is identical to **y**. We also need to know whether there is any entity **z** that is also psychologically continuous with **x**. Unless the proponent of the non-branching psychological theory can explain to us why we should reject the only x and y principle, it looks like the theory is in trouble.

3.3 Identity Doesn't Matter

The view that facts about personal identity are not fundamentally important – what we'll call the *Identity Doesn't Matter view* (or *IDM*, for short) – has been defended by various psychological continuity theorists, but perhaps its most prominent defender is Derek Parfit. For Parfit, IDM is combined with the non-branching requirement, and this is how the view has typically been developed. Adding the claim that identity doesn't matter to the non-branching requirement does not solve the problems for the non-branching requirement that we raised in the previous section. The proponent of this combination of views is still committed to the rejection of the only x and y principle. But, in claiming that facts about personal identity are not what matters, the proponent of IDM helps us to see why this perhaps should not worry us too much.

To help motivate IDM, it will be helpful to return to the case of distant transporter malfunction that we briefly considered above. In this scenario, after Margaret dematerializes on the transporter pad in London, Meg materializes in New York while Peg simultaneously materializes in New Zealand. Since personal identity requires non-branching psychological continuity, neither Meg nor Peg is identical with Margaret. But should this bother Margaret? Proponents of the IDM view think not. Rather, when Margaret looks ahead to the future, she should see that she has almost everything that she cares about with respect to continued existence, even though no one will exist who is identical with her.

For the moment, to make things simpler, let's suppose that almost immediately after Peg materializes in New Zealand there is a freak accident at the transporter facility there and she is instantly (and painlessly) killed. And now let's also suppose that, prior to stepping onto the transporter pad in London, Margaret is informed of everything that's about to happen. Perhaps technicians can predict when the transporter malfunctions will occur even though they can't prevent them, and perhaps the chain of events that will lead to the freak accident in New Zealand has already been put into motion. Let's not worry too much about how Margaret gets the information. Given what she knows, how should she think about her future?

Recall that Margaret's main priority as she steps onto the transporter pad in London is getting to see her father face to face before he dies. She wants to give him a kiss and tell him that she loves him. And of course, this is exactly what the woman who steps off the transporter pad in New York is going to do. Moreover, this woman not only looks exactly like Margaret but she feels like Margaret from the inside. She calls herself Margaret (though, to avoid begging questions about who deserves that name, we've been referring to her as Meg). She has the same memories, the same personality traits, the same interests as Margaret. She will interact with Mr. O'Malley exactly as Margaret would. From his perspective, there is no doubt that his daughter has come to visit. When she returns to London, she will pursue all of Margaret's projects exactly as Margaret would have. Doesn't the existence of this woman give Margaret everything that she wants for the future – or if not quite everything, isn't it still pretty close to exactly what she wants? Proponents of IDM claim that it is.

We often refer to people as surviving through their accomplishments: authors survive through their written works, architects survive through the buildings they've designed, and so on. Likewise we refer to parents as surviving through their children. Is this talk of survival merely metaphorical? If not, then these would be cases of survival without identity. So too, say proponents of IDM, we might think of Margaret's case as one of survival without identity. Though no one exists who is identical to her, she survives through the woman we've called Meg.

Now, let's add back in the complication we'd earlier avoided. Let's suppose that Peg is not killed after arriving in New Zealand but continues to exist. According to IDM, though Margaret is identical to neither Meg nor Peg, she survives through them both. This raises all sorts of complications. Suppose, for example, that Margaret is married with a son. Is Margaret's spouse now a bigamist? Has her son acquired an additional mother? Who is entitled to Margaret's savings? Who gets to keep Margaret's job? Who has to pay the parking ticket that Margaret received last week? There's no doubt that these questions would be very difficult to answer. But notice that the difficulties here are primarily *practical*, not metaphysical. For example, our legal system isn't prepared to deal with cases of duplicate survivors. In a world in which psychological continuity often branched, we would undoubtedly have to add some laws to the books to help us figure out how to handle these sorts of issues. Additionally, quite apart from legal matters, we would also have to adjust our social practices in such a world. Right now, we have no precedent for how duplicate survivors should interact with one another, or how other people should interact with them. Importantly, however, such changes to the law and to our social practices are not without precedent. Although there is no perfect analogy to the case of duplicate survivors, think about the kinds of changes that resulted from past struggles for equality – abolitionism, the women's suffrage movement, and so on.

For our purposes, the real question is not how these practical matters should be sorted out, but how this situation should best be viewed from Margaret's perspective. Should she see the result as no better than death? Proponents of the IDM view think not – or at least not generally speaking. Of course, there might be some cases in which an individual's life is so miserable that surviving in duplicate simply doubles the anguish she can anticipate in the future. But let's suppose that Margaret's life is not a miserable one. Why, then, shouldn't she be consoled by the fact that there's a real sense in which she manages to live on through Meg and Peg?

In fact, there might be some cases in which having duplicate survivors might be viewed as a benefit. Suppose, for example, that Margaret has for some time been feeling ambivalent about various aspects of her life. As much as she loves her spouse and her son, she also yearns to be unencumbered – to have the freedom to travel more, and to follow some of her other passions. Suppose also that she's recently received an attractive job offer in Hong Kong. Though she's very happy with her career in London, she is sorely tempted by the opportunities this new job would offer. Were this her situation, she might view the prospect of having duplicate survivors as an advantageous one, one in which both future life paths could be pursued. Meg could remain with her family and continue with the job in London while Peg could take off for single life at the job in Hong Kong. Granted, in neither case would *she* be the one pursuing these life paths. But she might regard this as a mere technicality. Her relationship to Meg and her relationship to Peg are just like the relationship she has with her future self, except for the duplication.

Parfit himself claims that he finds the truth of IDM both liberating and consoling. Before he came to this view, he writes: "I seemed imprisoned in myself. My life seemed like a glass tunnel, through which I was moving faster every year, and at the end of which there was darkness. When I changed my view, the walls of my glass tunnel disappeared. I now live in the open air" (Parfit 1984, 281). Nonetheless, many people, when confronted with this view, find it deeply unintuitive. Even proponents of the IDM view admit that it is a hard view to get oneself to believe. But, as they note, the fact that a view is hard to believe does not entail that it's untrue. Lots of facts that have been revealed to us by science are very hard to believe. To give just one example, Aristotle famously claimed that, were two objects of different weights dropped at the same time, the heavier object would fall faster than the lighter object. It's often said that Galileo proved Aristotle wrong by dropping two cannonballs of different sizes off the Tower of Pisa, but even if this story about Galileo is apocryphal, Aristotle's claim is demonstrably false (you can try it yourself). Nonetheless, many people continue to find this fact hard to believe even once alerted to the truth of the matter. Perhaps matters are similar with respect to IDM.

3.4 Fusion and Longevity

In the next and final section of this chapter, we will move on to consider four-dimensionalism, a version of the psychological theory that attempts to deal with the problem of reduplication by claiming that Meg and Peg pre-exist the transporter malfunction. Before doing so, however, it will be worth briefly considering some other cases that are often discussed in connection with the IDM view.

Though the reduplication problem arises when we think about cases involving *fission*, a related problem arises when we think about cases involving *fusion*. Insofar as fission sounded like mere science fiction, fusion may well sound even more incredible. But just as we can imagine alien races that are capable of fission, we can also imagine alien races that are capable of fusion. Consider yet another example from *Star Trek*, that of the alien species known as the Trill. As explained by Memory Alpha, a comprehensive *Star Trek* wiki:

> The Trill (or Trills) are a humanoid species native to the planet Trill. A small percentage of the Trill population co-exists with a sentient symbiotic organism known as a symbiont inside their bodies. The resulting joined Trills have personalities which are a synthesis of the two beings including the memories, and to some extent the personalities, of the previous hosts of the symbiont. (http://en.memory-alpha.org/wiki/Trill)

A joined Trill is thus a fusion between the Trill humanoid and the symbiont.

Alternatively, we might imagine a case of fusion with the aid of the transporter. If a transporter can malfunction and impose a single pattern twice, it seems that it could also malfunction by comingling two distinct patterns. We might imagine that John and Paul, both of whom need to get to London, step onto adjacent transporter pads in New York. But, due to a power surge at exactly the wrong moment, their patterns are mixed and only one individual materializes in London. This individual – let's call him JP – is both physically and psychologically a mixture of John and Paul. Some psychological traits are muted by the fusion: Paul's love for adventure is tempered by John's caution, for example, while John's hyper-punctuality is cancelled out by Paul's habitual lateness. Traits that they have in common, such as compassion, are amplified. Various other traits come together in different ways: Paul's passion for justice combined with

John's generosity gives rise to a deep sense of commitment to charitable giving.

From the perspective of John and Paul, what does this fusion amount to? Clearly JP is not identical to either of them. As we've seen, identity is a relation that holds one to one. But should they each think of themselves as surviving through JP? On *Star Trek*, the Trill do not regard being joined with a symbiont as equivalent to death. In fact, being joined is considered to be a great honor, and there is fierce competition among the Trill to become eligible for joining. But this Trill outlook might be wrong. Moreover, the relationship that John and Paul each have to JP is importantly different from the relationship that Margaret has to Meg and Peg. While Margaret has *complete* psychological continuity with both Meg and Peg, John and Paul each have only *partial* psychological continuity with JP.

Assessing this sort of case, Parfit concludes that survival is a matter of degree. What matters to us in survival may not be all or nothing. Some of the personality changes may be deeply regretted. But other personality changes that result from fusion might be welcomed. Perhaps, for example, Paul has been trying for years to be more punctual and John has always wanted to live life a little more "on the edge." Many people spend a lot of money on therapy and other treatments to rid themselves of undesirable habits and desires. (Perhaps fusion between a smoker and a non-smoker would turn out to be a very effective cure for nicotine addiction!) Moreover, we generally don't tend to regard personality changes as tantamount to death. Over the course of our natural lives, most of us go through many such changes – some of them dramatic ones. Someone might spend his teen years as a gang member in South Central Los Angeles before later becoming a minister who works tirelessly against gang violence. Someone else might start off as a Democrat who champions gun control before later becoming a Republican passionately committed to a citizen's right to bear arms.

Perhaps fusion is deeply impossible for human beings; maybe a transporter could not malfunction in the way we've imagined. But similar issues can also be raised by contemplating significant longevity. Recall from chapter 2 our discussion of Ray Kurzweil and his predictions that we will soon be able to merge with machines and thereby greatly extend our life spans, perhaps even becoming immortal. Writing in 2005, Kurzweil claims "We have the means right now to live long enough to live forever. Existing knowledge can be aggressively applied to dramatically slow down aging processes so we can still be in vital health when more radical life-extending therapies from biotechnology and nanotechnology become available" (Kurzweil 2005, 371). In fact, Kurzweil himself, born in 1948, is "aggressively reprogramming" his own biochemistry, taking 250 supplements a day and receiving several intravenous therapies each week, in an attempt to ensure that he will be around long enough to take advantage of these coming technologies.

But what would life be like at such a greater degree of longevity? At the age of 150, will Kurzweil still remember his childhood? What about at the age of 250? Or 350? Will he still have the goals and ambitions that he set for himself as a man of 50? Will any of his passions remain the same? It seems plausible to suppose that there will be many changes over time, some of them drastic. In such a case, if we ask whether Kurzweil has *really survived* to the age of 250, it might be hard to know what to say. Will it really still be Kurzweil *himself*? Notice here the problem is not that he's shed his original body – we're assuming that uploading preserves personal identity – but rather that the degree of psychological continuity that he has to his much younger self weakens over time.

On Parfit's view, such a case should not be seen as puzzling at all. Facts about identity are not always determinate. Though there are some cases in which the future being is obviously identical to Kurzweil, and some cases in which the future being is obviously not, there may also be some cases in between. In those cases, the question, "Will that future person be identical to Kurzweil?" simply has no answer. But, in Parfit's view, this should not concern us, since identity is not what matters in surivival. Moreover, psychological continuity – which *is* what matters to us in survival – comes in degrees. Thus, the higher the degree of psychological continuity that Kurzweil has to his future self, the more that Kurzweil will have of what matters in survival. Of course, just as it is difficult to believe the claim that identity is not what matters to us, it is also difficult to believe the claim that what does matter to us can be an issue of degree. Parfit himself admits that such claims are very hard to believe. In his opinion, however, the more we rehearse the arguments for the view, the more we can help to ease our doubts.

3.5 Four-Dimensionalism

Despite what Parfit says, I expect that some doubts will remain (and even Parfit admits that it may be hard to erase one's doubts entirely). So it may be helpful to know what our other options are. In this section, we review one prominent alternative: four-dimensionalism. Like proponents of the IDM view, four-dimensionalists deny that either Meg or Peg is identical to Margaret. But, unlike proponents of the IDM view, four-dimensionalists claim that both Meg and Peg existed prior to the transporter mishap. In order to understand this attempt to solve the problem of reduplication, we will first need some general background on the four-dimensionalist view.

Four-dimensionalism is a popular metaphysical view about the nature of objects' persistence through time. At the root of the theory is an analogy between space and time, or, more specifically, between an object's existence in space and an object's existence in time. We normally think of an object as having spatial parts. For example, my camera consists of many parts including a body, a battery casing, a lens, and a flash. It also consists of even smaller parts such as its atoms. According to the four-dimensionalist, objects also have temporal parts, what we can call *temporal stages*. So my camera has a 2013 stage and a 2014 stage among its many temporal parts. It also consists of smaller parts such as its July 2014 stage; its Wednesday, July 30, 2014 stage; or, even smaller than that, its 9:01 a.m. on Wednesday, July 30, 2014 stage. For the four-dimensionalist, persons work the same way. A person has spatial parts: I, for example, have a head, a torso, two arms, and two legs among my many spatial parts. And a person also has temporal parts: I, for example, have a 2010 stage and a 1990 stage among my many temporal parts. Typically, these temporal parts are referred to as *person-stages*.

We can carry this analogy further in various ways. At any given point of space, only part of an object is present. Likewise, at any given point of time, only part of an object is present. When I pick up my camera and hold it in my hands, I am not holding the whole camera – I am only holding its present temporal stage. So, for the four-dimensionalist, an object is not wholly present at any moment that it exists.

Four-dimensionalism contrasts with three-dimensionalism, a view that denies the existence of temporal parts. For the four-dimensionalist, an object persists through time by way of the existence of successive temporal parts. At any moment in time that it exists, it is present in virtue of the presence of one of its temporal parts. This kind of persistence through time is often referred to as *perdurance*. For the three-dimensionalist, an object persists through time by way of its existence at various times. At any moment in time that it exists, it is wholly and completely present. This kind of persistence through time is often referred to as *endurance*. As characterized by Ted Sider, a contemporary defender of four-dimensionalism: "a perduring object is 'spread out' over a region of spacetime, whereas an enduring object 'sweeps through' a region of spacetime, the whole of the object occupying the region's subregions at different times" (Sider 2001, 3).

On the four-dimensionalist view, then, we can think of objects persisting through time – including persons persisting through time – as spacetime worms. A person traces a worm-like path through space and time in virtue of the existence of its successive person-stages. Assuming that the four-dimensionalist takes the psychological approach, she will use the relation of psychological continuity to explain what makes two person-stages count as person-stages of the same person.

Or, to call on another analogy, we might consider a person's journey through time like a road's journey through space. (See Sider 2001, 2.) But sometimes two different roads might overlap for a stretch. I-95 is a major highway running up and down the east coast of the United States from Florida to northern Maine. Route 128, the Yankee Division Highway, forms a partial beltway around the city of Boston ending in Gloucester, Massachusetts. From Canton north to Peabody,

Route 128 runs concurrently along the same stretch of road as I-95. In Peabody, they diverge, with I-95 running north toward New Hampshire, and Route 128 running northeast to Gloucester. Between Canton and Peabody, then, the two roads share their spatial parts.

But if spatial parts can be shared, and time is like space, then the four-dimensionalist should also accept that temporal parts can be shared. On their view, this is precisely how we should best understand the relation of Margaret to Meg and Peg. From birth until the moment of the transporter malfunction, Meg and Peg share a path through time; they share all their temporal parts. At the moment of the transporter malfunction, the temporal paths traced by Meg and Peg begin to diverge, and they no longer share their temporal parts. The case of the transporter malfunction is thus, for the four-dimensionalist, not really properly thought of as a case of duplication or fission. Meg and Peg are not brought into existence by the transporter malfunction but rather have existed all along. Because they shared all of their temporal parts, however, their dual existence was hidden. Until the transporter malfunction, everyone who knew them unknowingly thought of them jointly as Margaret. It is only when the transporter malfunction occurs, and their temporal paths diverge, that they are revealed as distinct entities.

Four-dimensionalism thus faces what is often referred to as the *problem of overpopulation*: prior to the transporter malfunction, there are two persons in existence where we thought there was one. And, of course, the problem of overpopulation is even worse than we have already made out. Meg and Peg could also experience future transporter malfunction, presenting us with four individuals who trace their psychological continuity back to Margaret. So it was not just Meg and Peg sharing Margaret's temporal path all along. It was really all four individuals who did. And why stop there?

Things become even more problematic when we stop to think of this kind of situation from the first person perspective. Right now, I don't know whether I will ever experience any transporter malfunctions in the future. But if there is some transporter malfunction ahead of me, then that means that, right now, I am really a dual entity – even though I can't know it. When Margaret got into her car to head for the transporter station, there were really two people – Meg and Peg – sitting in the driver seat. Likewise, if I am going to experience fission at some point in the future, then there are really two people sitting in my chair right now. In fact, it's not even clear to whom I'd be referring when I use the word "I." Normally we think of "I" as referring uniquely to one's self – but if four-dimensionalism were true, words like "I" and "me" wouldn't seem to work this way.

Most readers undoubtedly find the problem of overpopulation deeply counterintuitive. Thus, though four-dimensionalism gives us a nice resolution to the problem of reduplication, we might think that it comes at too high a price. There is more to be said on behalf of four-dimensionalism – it plays an important role in resolving other deep-seated metaphysical problems – but it's nonetheless very hard to believe that there might be many distinct individuals sharing both your physical body and your psychological make-up without there being any way for you to determine this. On the other hand, the alternative solutions we've considered to the problem of reduplication are also pretty hard to believe. So we thus face a difficult choice. Either we find a way to make peace with one of these solutions, no matter how unsatisfying they might initially seem, or we abandon the psychological approach, despite all of its intuitive appeal. Unfortunately, as we will see in the next chapter, it is not clear that we will fare any better with an alternative approach. Since the correct theory of personal identity will likely require us to accept some counterintuitive results, it's worth thinking carefully about these options for the psychological theorist to see whether any of them present us with a bullet we are willing to bite.

Further Reading

Relevant excerpts from the correspondence between Clarke and Collins are reprinted in the useful anthology *Personal Identity*, edited by Perry (2008). Williams' development of the reduplication problem is found in several of his essays, most notably "Personal Identity and Individuation" (Williams 1956–7). For Parfit's development of the transporter case, see

Parfit (1984, chs. 10–14). An extended discussion and treatment of the reduplication problem can be found in Noonan (2003, ch. 7).

Lewis (1976) is a classic source for the development of a four-dimensionalist account of personal identity, though he does not refer to his view by that name. For a comprehensive discussion and defense of four-dimensionalism, see Sider (2001).

An excellent depiction of reduplication via transporter malfunction occurs in "Second Chances," an episode of *Star Trek: The Next Generation* (season 6, episode 24). In this episode, the crew of the *Enterprise* discover that an accident eight years earlier had led to the reduplication of crew member William Riker; one copy materialized on board his ship, while one copy materialized on Nervala IV, the planet he'd been visiting. For the past eight years, neither Riker knew of the existence of the other; one continued life in Star Fleet, one continued life marooned alone on the planet. Christopher Nolan's 2006 movie *The Prestige* – an excellent movie – is also highly relevant to the issues raised in this chapter (but I can't say why without spoiling the plot!).

4

The Physical Approach to Personal Identity

We began this book with a discussion of personhood that suggested the proper definition would likely be specified in terms of psychological capacities. The psychological theory of personal identity over time fits nicely with this conception. If persons are defined in terms of their psychology, then it would be natural for their identity over time to consist in some sort of psychological continuity. As we have seen, however, various problems arise with the psychological theory. The problems do not defeat the theory for there are several options for solutions available. But, at this point, it is worth considering whether there might be other plausible accounts of personal identity over time. In this chapter we consider several rivals to the psychological theory, all of which are versions of a physical approach to personal identity.

Central to the physical approach is the claim that our identity over time consists not in psychological facts but in physical facts. But which physical facts? Several different answers have been defended. One version of the physical approach – *the bodily theory* – holds that our identity over time consists in having the same body. Closely related to the bodily theory is a second version of the physical approach – *animalism* – which holds that our identity over time consists in our being the same biological organism over time. A third version of the physical approach – *the brain theory* – holds that our identity over time consists in having the same brain.

3 physical based theories

In this chapter, we will consider the advantages and disadvantages of each of these three competing versions of the physical approach. But before turning to look at them in more detail, we will start more broadly with some considerations used to support this general approach to personal identity.

4.1 Undercutting Intuitions

The case for the physical approach might be thought to begin with a defensive maneuver. As we have seen, proponents of the psychological theory tend to rely heavily upon various puzzle cases. When evaluating such cases, psychological theorists propose a compelling argument that our intuitive judgments count against the physical approach and in favor of the psychological theory. Proponents of the physical approach thus often feel the need to undercut these intuitions as a prelude to mounting a positive case for their own view. One particularly important attempt to do so comes from the work of twentieth-century English philosopher Bernard Williams. In "The Self and the Future," an influential paper from 1970, Williams argues that the standard presentations of the puzzle cases used by psychological theorists tend to unfairly color our judgments. To show this, he asks us to compare two different thought experiments. In what follows, though I've embellished some of the details of the thought experiments, the general line of argumentation comes directly from Williams.

To start, let's imagine a television reality show – *Swap Survivor* – in which two contestants voluntarily decide to undergo a procedure called The Swap for a chance at a $1 million prize. Of course, compelling television requires not only big rewards but also big risks – in this case, the risk of being briefly but very painfully tortured (though the network executives swear there will be no lasting bodily damage). Given that people have proved themselves to be willing to subject themselves to a multitude of horrors (such as being encased in a body bag filled with giant hissing cockroaches, flesh-eating worms, crickets, and stink beetles) for the comparatively paltry reward of $50,000 on *Fear Factor*, I have no doubt that the producers would be able to line up more than enough contestants for *Swap Survivor*.

The Swap is a procedure similar to others that we've previously considered – each contestant has his or her psychology downloaded from his or her brain, temporarily placed in a storage device, and then re-uploaded to the other contestant's brain. Once the Swap is performed, one of the contestants gets the prize and the other gets the torture. Who gets what is decided by random means. Let's suppose that this week's contestants are Aaron and Baron. Before undergoing the procedure, but after having been fully apprised of the details of The Swap, Aaron and Baron cast their votes for how they want the money and the torture to be allocated: should it go to the individual with Aaron's body/brain but Baron's psychology (for convenience, let's call him A.Bod) or the individual with Baron's body/brain but Aaron's psychology (let's call him B.Bod)?

Neither Aaron nor Baron is moved by altruistic concerns. Each sincerely wants to end up with the money. In this case, how should they vote? If they're both inclined toward the psychological theory, then presumably Aaron would vote for B.Bod to get the money while Baron would vote for A.Bod to get the money. If they're both inclined toward some kind of physical approach, then presumably Aaron would vote for A.Bod to get the money while Baron would vote for B.Bod to get the money. (Their theoretical preferences might also be split, but we can avoid that unnecessary complication.)

In either case, it looks like only one of the contestants will get what he voted for. Assume, for example, that in the big reveal near the end of the show, A.Bod wins the million-dollar prize. If both contestants had based their requests on the psychological theory, it seems reasonable to imagine that A.Bod, having Baron's memories, will remember having voted for this result and will be ecstatic with the outcome. Moreover, B.Bod, having Aaron's memories, will remember having voted for the other result, and he'll now be severely disappointed that things have worked out as they did. On the other hand, if they had each based their requests on some kind of physical approach, then it seems reasonable to imagine that A.Bod, having Baron's memories, will remember having voted for the other outcome but he'll now be elated that his vote was not honored. Conversely, B.Bod, having Aaron's memories, will be furious with himself for having requested this option, but he'll reluctantly admit that he got what he voted for. As this suggests, whichever way the contestants vote – whether they base their choices on the psychological theory or instead on some kind of physical approach – the *Swap Survivor* thought experiment ultimately generates intuitions for the psychological theory. However they felt beforehand, after the Swap each contestant identifies himself with the individual who has his psychology.

So far, we have a case that seems typical of the ones invoked by psychological theorists to support their view. But at this point, it's time to turn to a second puzzle case. Imagine that the evil scientist Dr. Mallie Volent has kidnapped an individual named Darren. As he sits in Dr. Volent's lair, handcuffed to a post, he learns that in about an hour he will be tortured. Quite understandably, this makes him extremely frightened, even terrified. Next, in the time-honored tradition of overly talkative evil scientists worldwide, Dr. Volent shares with Darren further details about her evil scheme:

> Before I torture you, I am first going to use my deprograminator on you. It's going to eliminate all of your memories, all of your beliefs, all of your bad habits, even all of your good habits. It will completely erase your mind. You won't even remember being told that you're going to be tortured. Once your brain is entirely wiped clean, I'm then going to reprogram you. I'll give you an entirely new set of memories, beliefs, and habits – some good and some bad. But don't worry, the deprograminator itself is completely painless. It's only after I've finished using it that the torture will commence.

How should Darren feel as he hears the details of Dr. Volent's evil scheme unfold? Here it seems natural that the proper reaction to each successive detail would be increasing fear. The fact that Darren is going to be both deprogrammed and then reprogrammed surely makes his situation even worse than it had seemed initially when he just had the torture to worry about. As he might now think to himself, "Not only am I going to be tortured, but I'm also going to have a complete psychological breakdown!"

Of course, however, what we have here is simply a different description of the previous thought experiment. Darren's predicament is simply that of the contestant of *Swap Survivor* whose body ends up being tortured. Importantly, however, the redescribed case generates a very different intuition. In this case, it looks like we side with some kind of physical approach – why else would Darren fear what is going to happen to his body after his psychology is gone from it? Thus, according to Williams, unless we can somehow invalidate the intuitions generated by this second thought experiment, there is no rational reason to endorse the psychological theory over some kind of physical approach. The thought experiments that seem to support it – and here we can generalize to transporter cases and uploads as well as transplants – cannot be trusted.

There are various lines of attack against Williams' argument. We might, for example, worry that the use of the second-person pronoun in the second version of the thought experiment means that it is described in non-neutral terms, perhaps even that it begs the question whether Darren is the one to experience the torture. We might also worry that the disappearance of Darren's own psychology makes an important difference. If a full version of The Swap occurs, Darren's psychology continues, while on Dr. Volent's evil scheme, it is never downloaded into another body. Both of these responses have some plausibility, and a proponent of the psychological theory might usefully pursue either one. But Williams' discussion is nonetheless a compelling one, and, at the very least, it reminds us that intuition may not be as clearly on the side of the psychological theory as its proponents would have us believe.

4.2   The Bodily Theory

Generally speaking, the way that we recognize and reidentify one another over time – our epistemological criterion for personal identity – depends crucially on our physical bodies. How can Inigo Montoya tell when he's finally found the individual who killed his father? The six-fingered right hand proves it: it's the master swordsman Count Rugen. How do we know that Voldemort's defeat comes by the wand of the same wizard he'd tried to kill as a baby? The lightning-shaped scar on the wizard's forehead proves it: It's Harry Potter.

According to the bodily theory, however, the body is not just a mere means for recognition and reidentification. Rather, the reason that we use bodies for these purposes is that our bodies constitute our identities. Each of us is identical to his or her body. Personal identity over time, on this view, thus consists in bodily identity over time:

> *The bodily theory*: A at time t1 is identical to B at some later time t2 if and only if A's body is numerically the same as B's body.

Interestingly, though the bodily theory is usually put forth as a theory of personal identity, proponents of the bodily theory often deny that they are giving a theory in terms of the technical notion of person that we developed in chapter 1. Judith Jarvis Thomson, a contemporary American philosopher who defends the bodily theory, notes that she is giving a theory of "just plain people – ordinary men, women, children, and infants" (Thomson 1997, 203). Thus, she claims, the fact that this view does not cohere well with the Lockean-inspired conception of personhood that we discussed previously is not supposed to count against it.

In addition to having the virtue of simplicity, the bodily theory seems to correspond with many of our ordinary intuitions about ourselves. Damage to my body is damage to *me*, not merely damage to a possession of mine. My left leg is not merely part of my body; it is part of *me*. But despite these points in its favor, the bodily theory has not been widely held. One problem stems from an inherent vagueness in the very notion of *same body*. This vagueness becomes apparent when we consider cases in which part of the body is damaged or even destroyed. When American snowboarder Amy Purdy had both of her legs amputated below the knee at the age of 19, was she left with numerically the same body? Or consider Taylor Morris, a member of the United States Navy trained to work with explosives. While stationed in Afghanistan in 2012, Taylor sustained serious injuries to all four of his limbs, ultimately losing both of his legs, his left arm from the bicep down, and also his right hand. After his accident, did he have numerically the same body? What about Marie Antoinette? When the guillotine was lowered on October 16, 1793, causing decapitation, was the headless body that remained still the same body?

We might also consider cases involving bodily transformations. When Rachel morphs into a bear in the Animorphs book series, does her bear form count as the same body as her human form? When Bruce Banner becomes the Hulk, does his body stay numerically the same? Related issues arise from cases involving bodily replacement parts. Presumably, a body will still be numerically the same even after a heart transplant, even if the heart were artificial. A body would also presumably be numerically the same even if it were also to get several more artificial transplants: kidneys, liver, and so on. But now consider an extreme case: if Raymond Kurzweil's predictions are correct, then within the next couple of decades we will begin to incorporate non-biological nanobot technology into our physical bodies. Consider someone who is an early adopter of this technology; let's call her Nan. After a period of time, 30 percent of her body has been replaced by nanobots and has thus become non-biological. Does Nan still have numerically the same body? What about at 50 percent? Or 100 percent?

Importantly, these cases do not show that personal identity comes apart from bodily identity. Rather, they are simply meant to show that we don't have a clear conception of what bodily identity amounts to. But this alone is enough to cause significant trouble for the bodily theory. As critics charge, "The notion of a human body is not clear enough to be of much use in discussing what it takes for us to persist" (Olson 1997, 149). Moreover, even if the bodily theorist were able to produce an adequate account of bodily identity, the theory faces another significant obstacle. In particular, it seems unable to accommodate our intuitive judgments in many of the cases we've so far considered. Most notably, perhaps, it fails to be able to account for intuitions in the upload and the brain transplant cases. Though it seems that I would survive if my consciousness is uploaded into a computer, in such a case I would no longer have any body at all. Thus, for the bodily theorist, uploading is tantamount to death. Likewise, when my brain is transplanted into someone else's body and my body is destroyed, most of us have the intuition that the surviving individual is me – let's call this *the transplant intuition*. But since the surviving individual has another person's body, the bodily theorist is again committed to claiming that I have ceased to exist.

Although the transplant intuition is very widely held – perhaps even nearly universally so (see Schechtman 2014, 152) – it's of course open to bodily theorists to simply reject it. Consider Gretchen Weirob, the fictional character from John Perry's *Dialogue on Personal Identity and Immortality* (1978) whom we mentioned briefly in chapter 2. As the dialogue takes place, Weirob is facing death. Though her mental faculties remain unimpaired, she has suffered grievous bodily injury as a result of a motorcycle accident, and her organs are now failing. Offered the opportunity to have her brain transplanted into another body, Weirob refuses. Weirob accepts that the survivor of the operation would not only seem to have her memories but would also take herself to be Gretchen Weirob. But, as Weirob notes, that alone is not enough for the survivor to be *her*. Someone suffering from a delusion might make the same judgment. And it would be not at all surprising that a procedure as complicated and delicate as the one involved in brain transplantation would have significant side effects. Why wouldn't delusion be among them?

Though Weirob is a fictional character, related worries have been expressed by real-life philosophers as well. According to Thomson, our intuitions about transplant cases are better seen as "merely openings for discussion, not closings" (Thomson 1997, 206). We need to take seriously the possibility that such intuitions might be mistaken. As we've already noted, the transplant intuition is supported by reflections on such a case from the first-person perspective. It seems to us that we can imagine waking up in a new body as a result of a brain transplant. But, says Thomson, how do we know that this is what we've really imagined? Suppose that right now I were to try to imagine myself switching bodies with Mary Pope Osborne, author of the Magic Treehouse books. To do so, I might close my eyes and imagine how things might look to me in such a situation. I imagine what life would be like if I were looking out at the world from Mary's eyes. And it seems easy to do so. I imagine myself looking down and seeing Mary's hands on a computer keyboard as she might see them were she to be looking down, or catching a glimpse of myself in a mirror and seeing Mary's face staring back at me. But, says Thomson, though it might be easy to produce these kinds of mental images, it's not clear that they should count as my having imagined what I set out to imagine: "how does my having formed that mental picture warrant my saying that I am imagining my having switched to Mary's body? There is nothing in the picture itself which could be thought to make it a picture of my having switched to Mary's body: the picture is merely a picture of Mary's body" (Thomson 1997, 218).

But even if Thomson is right that we should be wary of relying too heavily on our judgments about imagined cases, there are also real-life cases that count against the bodily theory. Consider the rare but real medical condition known as *dicephalus*, a special case of conjoined twinning in which a single body has two heads. The dicephalic twins Abigail and Brittany Hensel born in 1990 in Minnesota share a single body (one ribcage, two arms, one pelvis, two legs) with separate heads, brains, necks, and spinal cords. In the upper part of their body, they tend to have individual organs. For example, they each have their own heart, set of lungs, gallbladder, and stomach. Below the navel, they tend to share organs. For example, they share a bladder and colon and have only one set of reproductive organs. Since there is plausibly only one body here, the bodily theorist is committed to claiming there is only one person. But the twins do not share consciousness – each twin's thoughts are her own – and they have different personalities. Not only do they have different likes and dislikes, but also they often disagree with one another. The bodily theorist's assessment of this case thus seems highly counterintuitive. The claim that Abigail and Brittany are a single person does not speak to the reality of their lived experiences.

4.3   Animalism

In recent years, however, a view closely related to the bodily theory has also been much discussed. This view – sometimes called *the biological theory*, sometimes called *animalism* – eschews reliance on the notion of bodily identity. Rather, proponents of this view claim that we should focus on animal identity. As animals, human beings share the same kind of persistence conditions as other animals. But since not all animals even have psychological capacities at all – consider oysters, for example, or cockroaches – the conditions of animal identity over time cannot be specified in psychological terms. Rather, animal identity over time consists in a continuity of life-sustaining functions, or what we might call *biological continuity*:

(2) *Animalism*: A at time t1 is identical to B at some later time t2 if and only if there is biological continuity between A and B.

As even this brief description suggests, animalists tend to approach the problem of personal identity quite differently from psychological theorists. In particular, psychological theorists begin with the assumption that we are essentially persons. Animalists, in contrast, begin from the assumption that we are essentially animals. On the animalist view, though a human being may have the property of being a person, this should not be thought of as an essential property. Rather, it is more like the property "being a California resident" or the property "being a librarian" – a temporary property that can come and go. Even if you are presently a California resident, you could still be you at some later time without being a California resident. Likewise, even if you are at present a person, you could still be you at some later time without being a person. In a sense, then, the animalist thus does not really give a theory of *personal* identity over time but rather a theory of *animal* identity over time, and more specifically, the identity over time of animals like us. Relatedly, the animalist often quarrels with the very specification of the reidentification question that we have been working with. As we specified this question in chapter 2, it asks what makes a person the same person over time. In other words: What makes a person at one time identical to some future person? For the animalist, the reidentification question would be better stated more broadly: What makes a person at one time identical to some future existing being (person or not)?

Though the animalist view has its roots in the work of the ancient Greek philosopher Aristotle, the development of the theory has occurred relatively recently, primarily since the early 1990s. Proponents of the animalist approach include philosophers such as Paul Snowdon, Peter van Inwagen, and David Hershenov, but probably its most forceful defense has come via the work of philosopher Eric Olson. Olson's case against the psychological theory and for his own view is motivated in large part by two different sets of considerations. The first set is what's become known as *the fetus problem*. Consider Natasha, a pregnant woman, and her toddler son Jayden. Like many young kids, Jayden is very curious, and he keeps asking questions about his mother's expanding waistline. "You were once in Mommy's tummy too," Natasha tells him. She might even get out the pictures from her sonogram to show him. "See, that's you," she says, as she points at the grainy image. In doing so, Natasha assumes that Jayden was once a fetus. And this assumption seems entirely unquestionable. The problem, however, is that it does not seem compatible with the psychological theory.

Before the gestational age of about 24–28 weeks, a human fetus does not have any significant psychological capacities. It takes about that long for the cerebrum to develop sufficiently to be capable of supporting thought and sensation. There can thus be no psychological connections between Jayden and, say, the 16-week-old fetus that was once in Natasha's womb. As Olson notes, Jayden's "mental contents and capacities could not be continuous with those of a being with no mental contents or capacities at all"(Olson 1997, 73). Even later in pregnancy, once the cerebrum has developed its synaptic connections and is capable of supporting various mental functions, the fetus' brain is still not capable of forming memories or intentions or beliefs or desires. Since this precludes the possibility of psychological continuity between Jayden and that fetus – there can be no overlapping chains of connections of memories and intentions, and so on – the psychological view must deny that they are identical. On the psychological view, Jayden was never a fetus. And likewise for the rest of us.

We can capture the argument as follows:

1. I was once a fetus.
2. If the psychological theory is correct, then some relation of psychological continuity holds between me and some fetus who has once existed.
3. No relation of psychological continuity holds between me and any fetus that's ever existed.
4. Thus, the psychological theory is incorrect. *hence animalism*

Premise 2 seems to follow definitionally from the statement of the psychological theory, and premise 3 is factually hard to dispute. Thus, say the animalists, unless we are willing to reject premise 1, we should reject the psychological theory. Premise 1 is fully consistent with the animalist view. Because there is biological continuity between toddler Jayden and the fetus that was once in Natasha's womb, they are unquestionably the same animal.

Lurking in the background here might seem to be an even bigger problem: the infant problem. What kind of psychological continuity can Jayden have to the 1-day-old infant – or even the 1-month-old infant – that once slept in his bassinet? As Olson notes, it's unlikely that he can be "connected by a chain of overlapping memories or the like to a six-month-old infant; the child's brain simply lacks the capacity to remember or intend much of anything" (Olson 1997, 75). So, even if psychological theorists are willing to shrug off the worry about our identity with fetuses, it will be much harder to shrug off the worry about our identity with infants. The claim that "I was once an infant" seems even harder to deny than the claim that "I was once a fetus." That said, there might be a way for the psychological theorist to specify some kind of psychological continuity – perhaps continuity of psychological *capacity* – that enables each of us to be psychologically continuous with our infant selves, even if not our fetus selves. *fetal v. infant* Infants have developed certain psychological capacities that second-trimester fetuses still lack. For this reason, discussion has tended to focus on the fetus problem rather than the infant problem.

The fetus problem stems from issues related to the beginning of life, but there will also be parallel considerations stemming from issues related to the end of life, such as persistent vegetative states. Consider someone in such a state – call her Pearl – whose brain was deprived of oxygen, causing the destruction of the cerebral cortex. Since there might be varying degrees of persistent vegetative states, and since the term may be used differently by different people, let's simply stipulate that Pearl does not respond at all to external stimuli and it has been medically determined that all of her cognitive function has been irretrievably lost, i.e., there is zero chance that she will regain consciousness. Pearl thus has physical continuity with her former self but lacks any psychological continuity with that self. What do we say about such a case? It may be hard to sort out our intuitions here because the metaphysical issues are entangled with serious moral and legal concerns. Pearl is not legally dead, her will does not enter probate, the government does not consider her spouse to have been widowed, and so on. Moreover, we do not think that we can treat her any way we want. She still seems deserving of our moral consideration. But let's try to set aside these moral and legal issues. Is Pearl still lying in the hospital bed?

When considering this kind of case, the psychological theorist points out that we tend to think of the body lying in the hospital bed as an "empty shell," and we are likely to think that, in all the ways that matter, Pearl is already gone. In contrast, however, the animalist will point to a host of other considerations that suggest we consider Pearl still to exist. We still go to visit her. We spend a lot of money on her care. Moreover, suppose that you were to think prospectively about your own future and about what you would want to happen in such a situation. Preferences will undoubtedly come apart here. "If I were in that condition," some of you might think, "I hope my relatives would still come visit me." Others of you will probably have a different view: "If I were in that condition, I hope my relatives would pull the plug on me." On either preference, however, the fact that you'd tend to think of that future individual as *yourself* suggests a departure from the psychological theory and speaks in favor of a physical view like animalism.

In response to the fetus problem, proponents of the psychological theory will likely bite the bullet and accept that none of us were ever fetuses. But in doing so, they will also likely claim that this fact should not trouble us too much. Consider the fertilized egg from which Jayden came. Though he is not numerically identical to that fertilized egg, there was a process of growth that led from it to the person he now is. Likewise for the fetus. Though Jayden was not numerically identical to the fetus that was once in his mother's womb, there was a process of growth that led from it to the person he now is.

But even if proponents of the psychological theory can in this way overcome the fetus problem, animalists put forth a second set of considerations – *the thinking animal argument* – to make the case for animalism. Though the problem was originally introduced by Snowdon (1990), it has recently been forcefully developed by Olson:

> It seems evident that there is a human animal intimately related to you. It is the one located where you are, the one we point to when we point to you, the one sitting in your chair. It seems equally evident that human animals can think. They can act. They can be aware of themselves and the world. Those with mature nervous systems in good working order can, anyway. So there is a thinking, acting human animal sitting where you are now. But you think and act. You are the thinking being sitting in your chair. It follows from these apparently trite observations that you are an animal. (Olson 2003a, 325)

The argument can be captured as follows:

1. There is a human animal located where you are right now (say, in your chair).
2. That human animal is thinking.
3. You are the thinking being in your chair.
4. Therefore, you are a human animal.

Though this argument clearly supports animalism, it may not be immediately apparent why it would count against the psychological theory. According to Olson, however, the psychological theorist cannot accept the claim that each of us is a human animal. Since the psychological theory allows for cases where there will be the same person but not the same animal, personal identity comes apart from animal entity.

Consider again the brain transplant case. According to the psychological theorist, when Brian's brain is transplanted into Bodie's body, the resulting individual with Brian's brain and Bodie's body is Brian. But, as Olson says, "we don't transfer any *animal* from one head to another" when we perform this transplant. Rather, "we transplant an organ from one animal to another"(Olson 1997, 94). So this resulting individual – which on the psychological theory is the same person as Brian – is not the same animal. When the transplant occurs, Brian left behind not only his original body but also, as we might say, his original animal. As this suggests, the psychological theorist views our relationship to our animals like our relationship to our bodies. Just as you may temporarily occupy a body, you may temporarily occupy an animal. But just as you are not identical to the body you temporarily occupy (you can't be identical to it if you can leave it behind), you also are not identical to the animal you temporarily occupy (again, you can't be identical to it if you can leave it behind). You are not your body, and you are not your animal.

To avoid the conclusion of the thinking animal argument, the psychological theorist must deny one of the argument's three premises. To deny premise 1 – to deny that there is a human animal sitting in the chair where you are sitting – looks tantamount to the denial of the existence of human animals altogether. And that seems wildly implausible. To deny premise 2 – to deny that the human animal sitting in the chair is thinking – looks tantamount to the denial that human animals can think. That also seems implausible. But suppose we accept the first two premises – we accept that there is a human animal sitting in the chair, and we accept that it is thinking. Might the psychological theorist deny premise 3? Assuming that she doesn't want to deny that you are a thinking being, then it looks as though she would have to deny that you're the only thinking being present in the chair. Just as it would be false to say that Ron Weasley is *the* brother of Ginny Weasley – since Ginny has more than one brother, Ron is just one of many – it would be false to say that you are *the* thinking being in that chair: the chair has more than one thinking being in it, and so you are just one of many. It's for this reason that the thinking animal argument is often referred to as the *too-many-thinkers problem*.

Of course, in saying that there's more than one thinker in the chair, the psychological theorist would not be saying that you're sitting on someone's lap, or that someone else is sitting on your lap. Rather, she'd be saying that there are two (or more) coincident entities in the chair, entities that occupy the same space at the same time. As we've seen, however, this is exactly the kind of claim that a four-dimensionalist is committed to. In fact, the too-many-thinkers problem is directly analogous to the problem of overpopulation that we encountered in chapter 3. Thus, a psychological theorist could respond to the too-many-thinkers problem by adopting four-dimensionalism. Although the commitment to coincident entities and the resulting overpopulation may still strike us as unintuitive, the fact that four-dimensionalism provides a unified way of responding to various worries that we've encountered is a point in its favor.

Alternatively, a psychological theorist might respond to the problem by trying to undercut the soundness of the thinking animal argument itself. Directly parallel to such an argument is the following:

1. There is a human head located where you are right now (say, in your chair).
2. That human head is thinking.
3. You are the thinking being in your chair.
4. Therefore, you are a human head.

And a similar case could be made for a human head-and-neck, a human upper body, and so on. If these arguments were good ones, then it would follow that you are identical not only with a human animal, but also with a human head, and with a human head-and-neck, and with a human upper body... But since these things are not identical to each other, you can't be identical to them all. Thus, unless the animalist can provide us with some explanation for why you should be identified with the human animal and not with the human head, we can reject the thinking animal argument. (For further discussion, see Blatti 2014.)

As we've seen in this section, animalism makes sense of two of our deep-seated intuitions about ourselves: that we were once fetuses, and that we are thinking animals. These

[margin note:] obj: how can we be human animal v human head

are important advantages of the theory. But the view also has some significant drawbacks. Like the bodily theorist, the animalist cannot account adequately for cases of dicephalus. Not only do Abigail and Brittany Hensel share a body but, given that their organs work together in a single, fully integrated functional system, it also seems that there is only one human organism between them. Thus, the animalist is committed to the implausible claim that they are a single individual. Also like the bodily theorist, the animalist must reject our intuitive judgments in both upload and transplant cases. It's probably obvious why the animalist must deny the upload intuition, since a brain uploaded into a non-biological machine or android body would not be a human organism at all. But it might be less obvious why, for the animalist, the individual that would result were your brain to be transplanted into another body would not be you. To see this, it may be helpful to consider a slightly amended version of the transplant case that we've previously considered. Suppose that the neurosurgeons transplant not your whole brain into another body but just your cerebrum, the part of your brain responsible for consciousness. Even without a cerebrum, the being that remains would still be able to sustain life functions. Essentially, it would be in a persistent vegetative state. For the animalist, because the remaining being is biologically continuous with you, since it is still the same human organism, that remaining being is you – and this is true despite the fact that there is now another body with your cerebrum and consciousness. Thus, like bodily theorists, animalists must reject the transplant intuition. Interestingly, Olson does not try to discount the force of that intuition and explicitly admits that he feels its pull. On his view, however, our other intuitions end up trumping this one. His sense that he's a human organism carries more weight.

Where does this leave us? Clearly, the animalist view has some counterintuitive consequences. But, as we've seen, the psychological theory looks as though it is committed to some unintuitive claims as well. In fact, since our intuitions seem to pull us in different directions, it's hard to see how a successful theory could accommodate them all. Any theory, then, is likely to have to bite the bullet somewhere. Where the theories differ is on which bullet is easiest to bite.

4.4 The Brain Theory

By this point, some of you will undoubtedly be impatiently awaiting discussion of the brain theory, a view that has significant intuitive plausibility. Since the brain is what's responsible for psychological continuity, this theory shares many of the advantages of the psychological theory while at the same time accommodating intuitions that we are physical beings.

In recent years, American philosopher Jeff McMahan has developed a version of the brain theory that he refers to as the *embodied mind theory*. For McMahan, our continued existence depends on our having the same consciousness or, as he often puts it, the same mind. But minds are embodied in brains, and so McMahan ultimately concludes that a person's continued existence consists in the continued existence and functioning of enough of the same brain to be capable of generating consciousness. To put this more precisely:

The embodied mind theory: A at time t1 is identical to B at some later time t2 if and only if there is sufficient non-branching physical and functional continuity between A's brain and B's brain to preserve certain basic psychological capacities, particularly the capacity for consciousness.

Several aspects of this view need clarification. First, in specifying when a brain will count as having sufficient functional continuity, McMahan requires only that the brain support continuity of psychological *capacity* and not continuity of psychological *content*. As McMahan notes, the functional continuity of those areas of the brain responsible for consciousness usually supports broad psychological continuity, "but in the very earliest phases of an individual's life and in some instances near the end, the same mind or consciousness persists in the absence of any degree of psychological connectedness from day to day" (McMahan 2002, 68). Second, it is important to note that McMahan's account requires not only the functional continuity of the brain but also physical continuity. Physical continuity for McMahan does not require sameness of constituent matter, but it does require that any change to the constituent matter be gradual and incremental.

Though the cells in the brain do not undergo continual replacement, like the cells in the skin, McMahan's account of physical continuity would not rule out a brain's continued existence as the same brain if parts of it were replaced. As long as any such replacement was gradual and incremental, not sudden and complete, the brain's physical continuity remains.

With these clarifications in place, it will be useful to consider three related cases involving the loss of psychological capacities:

- *Persistent vegetative states.* First let's recall Pearl, an individual in a persistent vegetative state who has irretrievably lost the capacity for consciousness.
- *Deep coma.* Let's also consider Earl, who is in a deep coma as a result of having suffered damage to the reticular formation, an area in the brainstem that controls arousal in the cerebral hemispheres. Although the parts of Earl's brain responsible for consciousness remain intact, they remain dormant. As McMahan describes such a case, "It is as if the person is asleep but cannot be waked. All aspects of his mind are preserved intact in the tissues of his cerebral hemispheres, but their arousal is impeded by a defect in a critical support system" (McMahan 2002, 449).
- *Alzheimer's disease.* Finally, let's consider Merle, who is in an advanced stage of Alzheimer's disease and suffers from severe dementia.

According to both the bodily theory and animalism, all three of these individuals continue to exist. In each case, there is both bodily and biological continuity. In contrast, according to the psychological theory, none of these individuals continues to exist. In each case, there has been an extensive – perhaps even total – break in psychological continuity. Note that while these theories disagree on their assessment of the three cases, they nonetheless agree that we should treat all three cases the same way.

On the embodied mind theory, however, there are important differences between the three cases, to which we need to attend. With respect to persistent vegetative states, the embodied mind theorist agrees with the psychological theorist that the person has ceased to exist. Although the brain in such cases may retain its physical continuity, there has been a significant disruption in its functional continuity. There is no longer any capacity for consciousness, even in principle. With respect to deep comas, however, the embodied mind theorist disagrees with the psychological theorist and sides instead with the bodily theorist and animalist. In the deep coma, there is a sense in which the capacity for consciousness still exists, even though it cannot be activated. Thus, a person in a deep coma has not ceased to exist. Finally, with respect to Alzheimer's disease, McMahan thinks we need to distinguish between different phases of the disease, even once it has reached an advanced stage and severe dementia has set in. An individual suffering from severe dementia will lack continuity of psychological *content*. But as long as the continued functioning of the brain allows for continuity of psychological *capacity*, that will be enough to ensure personal identity on the embodied mind theory. It's only once the disease has progressed to such a point that the individual's brain no longer supports even the capacity for consciousness that the embodied mind theorist will claim that the person has ceased to exist. At that point, as with the case of an individual in a persistent vegetative state, all that is left is an empty shell.

We can now also see more generally how McMahan's view handles the various puzzle cases and problems that we have been discussing. First, unlike bodily theorists or animalists, but like the psychological theorist, the embodied mind view can easily accommodate the transplant intuition. When Brian's brain is transplanted into Bodie's body, the resulting individual is Brian. Although the brain is now in a different body, it retains both its functional and its physical continuity throughout the transplant procedure. Second, McMahan's view also leads to a more satisfying treatment of dicephalus than those of the bodily theory and animalism. Though Abigail and Brittany Hensel share a body, and though there seems to be only one human organism, they have different brains, each of which supports distinct minds. Thus, for the embodied mind theorist, as for the psychological theorist, Abigail and Brittany are distinct persons.

When it comes to teleportation, however, the embodied mind theory gives a less satisfying result. When Margaret steps on the transporter pad in London, she has no physical continuity to the person who materializes in New York. Since McMahan requires not only functional continuity of the brain but also physical continuity, the embodied mind view must hold that the person who materializes in New York – even when the transporter is working perfectly well – is not Margaret. On his view, then, teleportation is not a means of travel but is equivalent to death. McMahan also has to deny the upload intuition. Uploading one's consciousness to a computer severs the physical and functional continuity of the brain. On his view, then, futurists like Kurzweil are mistaken in thinking that they can extend their lives indefinitely by way of uploading. Without the brain, continued existence is impossible.

The fetus problem also poses something of a threat to the embodied mind theory. But while the psychological theorist must deny that we were ever fetuses of any gestational age, the embodied mind account need only deny that we were once first- and second-trimester fetuses. As we noted earlier, the brain of a fetus develops the capacity for consciousness somewhere between 24 and 28 weeks of pregnancy. Prior to that, the brain has not yet developed the structure and organization needed to support consciousness. Thus, on the embodied mind view, each of us comes into existence at approximately the beginning of the third trimester. This is undoubtedly still somewhat counterintuitive. The sonogram picture that Natasha shows her son Jayden, for example, might well have been taken in the second trimester, and yet we are still inclined to think that it's a picture of him. But the fetus problem seems less threatening to the embodied mind theorist than it does to the psychological theorist.

Ultimately, then, there is much that is attractive about the embodied mind account. It retains many of the advantages of the psychological theory while accommodating the intuition that something about our physical nature matters for our continued existence. It is also able to avoid many of the counterintuitive consequences of the other versions of the physical theory. For many people, however, its inability to accommodate the possibility of survival by teleportation or by uploading will be a decisive mark against it. Though McMahan is undoubtedly right that the brain typically has importance in our identity over time, ultimately that importance seems derivative of its normal role in preserving psychological continuity. Consideration of cases in which there is psychological continuity without the same brain – as in the cases of uploading and teleportation – tends to show that brain continuity in and of itself does not seem to be required for personal identity over time.

4.5 The Problem of Multiplicity

Thus far, our discussion in this chapter has primarily focused on the advantages and disadvantages of the different versions of the physical approach. But before closing our discussion of physical theories, it is worth considering a more general sort of problem that all such theories face: what I'll call *the problem of multiplicity*. There are various phenomena – most notably that of dissociative identity disorder – in which several persons seem to share a single physical manifestation – a single organism, body, and brain. In this section, we will look at this problem in more detail.

According to the American Psychiatric Association, dissociative identity disorder (DID) – which until 1994 was referred to as *multiple personality disorder* – is one of a cluster of several dissociative disorders. When an individual suffers from such a disorder, the normally integrated functioning of consciousness, memory, identity, and/or perception is disrupted. As characterized by the most recent version of the *Diagnostic and Statistical Manual of Mental Disorders*, the diagnostic criteria for DID describe it as a "disruption of identity characterized by two or more distinct personality states... The disruption of identity involves marked discontinuity in sense of self and sense of agency." Such a condition is also marked by "recurrent gaps in the recall of everyday events, important personal information, and/or traumatic events that are inconsistent with ordinary forgetting" (American Psychiatric Association 2013, 292).

The different personality states – which used to be referred to as "personalities" but are now more commonly referred to as "alters" – each has executive control of the body at different times. Sometimes alters have no consciousness of what occurs when they do not have bodily control, while sometimes they claim to have a continuing existence even when a different personality is in charge of the body. Though early cases of DID tended to involve just two or three alters, more recently the typical cases seem to involve six to sixteen. Alters can differ dramatically from one another, and such differences run along a great variety of dimensions. Different alters not only differ from one another with respect to personality traits but may also differ with respect to factors such as gender, allergic reactions, handedness, sensitivity to medicine, and the need for eyeglasses. (See Braude 1991, ch. 2, for a more complete survey of these differences.)

One case of DID that has been frequently discussed in the philosophical literature concerns a woman referred to pseudonymously as Christine Beauchamp (pronounced *Beecham*). Beauchamp's case was extensively documented and analyzed by Morton Prince, an influential American physician and psychologist who worked in the late nineteenth and early twentieth centuries. His book on this case, *The Dissociation of a Personality* (1905), is widely considered a classic in abnormal psychology.

According to Prince, Beauchamp's childhood had been a difficult one. Her mother, who died when she was 13, was neglectful. Though Prince is circumspect in relating what happened to her in the years after her mother's death, his account strongly implies that she was abused by her father. (In general, DID is strongly associated with abuse in childhood.) At the age of 16 she ran away from home and eventually took up a job as a nurse. When Prince first met Beauchamp in 1898, she was a nervous, reticent 23-year old woman in poor health. Increasingly unable to function in everyday life, she suffered from insomnia, fatigue, headaches, and depression. During the course of her treatment, Prince encountered three distinct alters whom he thought of informally as The Saint, The Devil, and The Woman (Prince 1905, 16). The first alter, whom he referred to as B1, was very religious and conscientious; she was hardworking, and she loved books and needlecraft. The second alter, who adopted the name "Sally" for herself, was mischievous and considerably more coarse. She was not as well educated as B1, hated books, and liked to drink and smoke. The third alter was referred to by Prince as B4, though Sally referred to her as "the Idiot." More courageous and ambitious than B1, she was also considerably more self-interested.

Not only did the alters have different personality traits, but they also had different skills. While B1 could speak French, for example, Sally could not. B4 and Sally were considerably healthier than B1, both mentally and physically, with Sally the healthiest of the three. They also had different tastes. While B1 liked milk and vegetables and preferred her lemonade with sugar, B4 disliked both milk and vegetables and strongly preferred unsweetened lemonade. The differences among the alters naturally led to difficult situations. B4 would often wear clothing so tight that it would cause B1 extreme discomfort. Likewise, B1 would become nauseated from the effects of Sally's cigarettes. Sally's prankster tendencies also led to trouble for B1. She would spend B1's money and destroy her knitting projects, sometimes elaborately so. Knowing B1's aversion to spiders, Sally also once wrapped some up in a pretty parcel and left it for B1 to open upon returning to control of the body.

The specific details of the interactions among Beauchamp's alters are simply fascinating, and much more could be recounted here. But, at this point, we hopefully have enough of the details before us to take up the question that primarily interests us: Do these three alters constitute three different persons? As a psychologist, not a philosopher, Prince himself was primarily concerned with the treatment of his patient. The question with which he was primarily occupied was thus: Which of these alters represents the real Christine Beauchamp? But insofar as Prince does address the issue of counting persons, he seems to take each alter to be a distinct person. Consider how he first introduces the case to us:

Miss Christine L. Beauchamp, the subject of this study, is a person in whom several personalities have become developed. ...In addition to the real, original or normal self, the self that was born and which she was intended by nature to be, *she may be any one of three different persons.* I say three different, because, although making use of the same body, each, nevertheless, has a distinctly different character; a difference manifested by different trains of thought, by different views, beliefs, ideals, and temperament, and by different acquisitions, tastes, habits, experiences, and memories. (Prince 1905, 1; emphasis added)

Many of the contemporary philosophers who have explicitly taken up the Beauchamp case – or the case of DID more generally – agree with Prince. Kathleen Wilkes, after an extensive discussion of the Beauchamp case, ultimately concludes that the evidence best supports the judgment that there were three persons – B1, Sally, and B4 – occupying a single body (Wilkes 1988). Having also attended closely to the Beauchamp case, philosopher Jennifer Radden agrees. In her view, the only way adequately to explain the "often contradictory and puzzling behavior" associated with DID is to postulate two or more distinct persons (Radden 1996, 52). Likewise, American psychologist and lawyer Elyn Saks – who herself battles schizophrenia – has argued that the claims that personalities are persons is "philosophically plausible." Reviewing the empirical evidence that supports this tentative conclusion, Saks notes that alters "differ characterologically, have distinct senses of self, perceive fellow alters to be separate people, see the world from a first-person perspective, possess unique life histories and memories, take control of their bodies, and evince unique physiological responses" (Saks 2000, 50). Other philosophers who have argued for a similar conclusion include Dennett (1976) and Shoemaker (2009).

Despite the widespread support for this conclusion, the view that DID presents us with distinct persons is not without its detractors. In fact, many mental health professionals working with DID patients deny that the different alters are different persons. Colin Ross, a leading DID researcher, claims that the different alters are best understood as rather fragmented parts of one person (Ross 1994, ix). Likewise, the psychiatrist Frank Putnam claims that "whatever an alter personality is, it is *not* a separate person" (Putnam 1989, 103). However, as persuasively argued by the philosopher

Stephen Braude (1991), such characterizations can be misleading. In particular, it is not clear whether such researchers
are working with the philosophical sense of person that we
have been employing throughout our discussion.

Furthermore, even if one is skeptical that DID itself presents us with a case in which several persons are housed in a
single body, reflection on the phenomenon suggests that there
is no conceptual incoherence in imagining such a case. As
Radden notes, even if our normal descriptions of DID itself
are misleading or exaggerated, we have "sufficient reason to
acknowledge that something like the phenomenon as
described may be empirically possible" (Radden 1996, 54).
One real-life example comes as a result of commissurotomy,
a neurosurgical procedure designed to sever the corpus cal-
losum, i.e., the membranes connecting the brain's two hemispheres. Commissurotomies were performed in the middle of
the twentieth century in the hopes of treating severe epilepsy.
The patients on which they were performed – often referred
to as *split brain patients* – functioned more-or-less normally
in everyday life, but in certain experimental procedures were
discovered to have what appeared to be two different centers
of consciousness and hence, perhaps, to be two different
persons. Another possible example comes from cases of
spiritual possession of a psychic medium "channeling" other
personalities. If we can make conceptual sense of these phenomena, then they might also show the possibility that
persons need not correspond to bodies and brains in a 1:1
ratio.

As our discussion thus far should make clear, the problem
of multiplicity poses a threat to all versions of the physical
approach. In such cases, we have a single body, a single
human organism, and a single brain. But we seem to have
multiple persons. Thus, personal identity seems to come apart
from the relevant physical facts and cannot be said to consist
in them. While the psychological theory can nicely accommodate multiplicity, the phenomenon poses a problem for
any version of the physical theory.

A bodily theorist like Thomson might respond to the
problem of multiplicity by reminding us that she is not giving
a theory of personal identity in the technical philosophical
sense of "person." This thus allows her to admit that the

Beauchamp case involves three persons in the technical sense of the term, while denying that there are three people in the ordinary sense of the term. To my mind, however, this response is implausible. Even if we grant that the ordinary notion of "person" is different from the philosophical notion of "person," it is not just philosophers who have the sense that there is multiplicity in cases of DID. Recall, for example, that the psychologist Prince claimed that Beauchamp was constituted by three different persons. The multiplicity with which we are confronted in cases of DID relates not only to the technical philosophical concept of "person" but also to the ordinary notion as well.

What might the brain theorist say in response to the apparent multiplicity in cases like DID? McMahan himself explicitly refrains from considering the phenomenon: "I will not comment on [DID]; there is as yet insufficient understanding of what actually goes on in these cases, and in particular little understanding of the neurological bases of the disorder" (McMahan 2002, 87). Though McMahan is surely right that there is much we still don't know about DID, the discussion in this section suggests that the how-many-persons question must be taken seriously. Moreover, as we've already noted, even if it turns out that the best explanation of DID does not require us to posit distinct persons, the presence of more than one person in a single body, sharing a single brain, still seems conceptually possible.

In defending animalism, however, Olson has recently tried to deny precisely this point. On his view, the phenomenon of multiplicity is not possible, even in principle. No matter how deep a personality split might appear, there could never be more than one individual like us sharing a single brain. As he puts it, "there is simply no room for two of us within one human being" (Olson 2003b, 329). Perhaps a brain theorist like McMahan could offer a similar sort of argument. But our intuition that multiplicity is possible is not easily given up. When we read a story like Stevenson's *Dr. Jekyll and Mr. Hyde*, we don't dismiss the story on the grounds that its central plot element doesn't make any sense. Thus, whatever the right analysis of DID turns out to be, it remains the case that the problem of multiplicity poses a significant threat to physical theories of any sort.

Further Reading

A defense of the physical theory can be found in several papers by Williams (1956–7, 1960, 1970). A defense of the body theory can be found in the work of Thomson (1997). McMahan's brain theory is developed in detail in his *The Ethics of Killing* (2002); see also Nagel (1986). Blatti provides a helpful introduction to animalism in his *Stanford Encyclopedia of Philosophy* entry on the topic (2014). A comprehensive development and defense of the theory comes in Olson (1997); a shorter discussion comes in Olson (2003a).

For useful discussions of DID and the problem of multiplicity, see Wilkes (1988) and Radden (1996). Nagel's classic paper "Brain Bisection and the Unity of Consciousness" (Nagel 1971) explores in detail the problem of multiplicity arising from the case of split brain patients. Olson (2003b) presents an animalist response to the problem of multiplicity. *The United States of Tara*, an American television series that aired on Showtime from 2009 to 2011, centers around a suburban housewife and mother who is diagnosed with DID.

5
From Reidentification to Characterization

As with many problems in philosophy, the question of our identity over time has proved remarkably difficult to answer. None of the views that we've considered so far proves to be wholly satisfactory, and there is not a clear consensus among professional philosophers about which approach is correct. In a survey conducted in 2009 of over 900 philosophy professors at leading universities throughout the English-speaking world, 34 percent claimed that they accepted or leaned toward some kind of psychological approach, 17 percent claimed that they accepted or leaned toward some kind of physical approach, and 12 percent claimed that they accepted or leaned toward the further fact view. The remaining 37 percent either were undecided, didn't feel they knew enough to answer the question, or accepted another view. When these same 900+ philosophers were asked their intuitions about the kind of teleportation case that we've considered (in which the person who arrives at the destination does not have the same physical mater as the person who stepped onto the transporter pad), 36 percent indicated that they thought the person would survive, while 31 percent thought that teleportation of this sort amounted to death. Again, the remaining 33 percent either were undecided, didn't feel they knew enough to answer the question, or accepted another view (Bourget and Chalmers 2014).

Thus, while twice as many of the philosophers surveyed accept the psychological approach as accept the physical approach, the large number of philosophers in the "other" category means that the psychological approach is preferred by only about a third of survey respondents. This is far from decisive support.

At this point in our discussion, there are two reactions that I think it would be natural to have. First, one might become convinced that we should give up on both the psychological approach and the physical approach altogether and find some entirely different approach. Alternatively, one might become convinced that the reason we are having so much trouble determining the answer to the reidentification question is that there is simply no answer. In this chapter, we will look at both of these reactions in more detail. As we will see, despite the naturalness of these reactions, both of them should ultimately be rejected. But exploring them more closely nonetheless enables us to make some progress on the problem of personal identity.

5.1 The Further Fact View = identity ϕ be reduced

Both the psychological theory and the physical theory are reductionist theories; they attempt to reduce claims about personal identity to other facts (either psychological facts or physical facts, respectively). In contrast, the further fact view is a non-reductionist view. On this view, personal identity cannot be reduced to other facts. Rather, it is a further fact over and above the psychological and physical facts. Perhaps it is a fact about a purely mental entity, such as a non-physical soul or some other purely spiritual substance. Perhaps it is a fact that is in some way consistent with the claim that we are purely physical beings. For example, on Lynne Rudder Baker's view, personal identity is understood in terms of the persistence of a single first-person perspective (see, e.g., Baker 2007, 2012). Though this persistence is irreducible to physical or psychological facts, Baker takes her view to be wholly compatible with the claim that persons are essentially embodied. But, however the further fact view is developed, what's central to the view is the claim that the fact of personal identity holds independently of all of the psychological and physical facts. On this view, personal identity is ultimate and unanalyzable.

For simplicity, let's consider a proponent of the further fact view who believes that the relevant further fact concerns nonphysical souls. Such a view seems to have been held by both Butler and Reid, whose views we encountered previously when we were considering objections to Locke's memory theory. More recently, it has been endorsed by contemporary philosophers such as Richard Swinburne and Geoffrey Madell.

Two sets of considerations are often raised in support of the further fact view. First, such a view seems to be the only view capable of giving us an account of personal identity in the *strict and philosophical* sense of identity, as opposed to merely the *loose and popular* sense of identity. Suppose that, several decades ago as a child, I used to love to climb the young oak tree in my backyard. Now, upon returning to my childhood home, I look upon the mature oak tree with fondness. In our ordinary way of talking, the oak tree that I'm looking at now is the *very same* oak tree as the one I climbed as a child. Though its leaves have fallen and regrown many times, and though it has added and lost branches, it has remained there all along with no excavation or replanting having been done. Importantly, however, there is no reason to believe that the oak tree now standing on that spot shares even a single particle of matter with the oak tree of several decades ago. According to Butler, this means that our loose, ordinary way of talking departs from the strict, philosophical facts: "if they have not one common particle of matter, they cannot be the same tree, in the proper philosophic sense of the word same; it being evidently a contradiction in terms, to say they are, when no part of their substance, and no one of their properties, is the same" (Butler 1736, 101). Talk of sameness of body will fall prey to a similar argument, and likewise for talk of sameness of consciousness. Really, what we call the same consciousness is a successive series of similar but strictly different consciousnesses. As the proponent of the further fact view concludes, the only way for there to be personal identity in the strict and philosophical sense is for there to be an unchanging substance, e.g., a non-physical soul.

The second set of considerations stems from thinking about the special concern we each have for our own futures: what is often called *egoistic* concern. Note that "egoistic" here does not mean "egotistic" – in having concern for one's future self one need not be narcissistic or inappropriately selfish. Rather, it's just that each of us naturally and unproblematically cares deeply about what happens to us in the future. In my case, for example, I dread the dentist's appointment I have scheduled next week, and I look forward to the vacation I'll soon be taking to Hawaii. I worry about how long I'll continue to feel this pain in my right knee. I hope that I will live long enough to see my children graduate from college and have children of their own – and so on. Of course, I also care deeply about all sorts of other people – about my spouse, my children, my friends – but the concern I have for myself is special. It differs in kind from the concern I have for others. Having egoistic concern seems both natural and reasonable, so much so that it is hard to imagine what a person who lacked any such concern would be like. According to the proponent of the further fact view, however, neither the psychological theory nor the physical theory can make sense of our egoistic concern. Only if we accept the existence of the further fact can such concern be rationally justified.

This objection dates back at least to Butler, who argued that Locke's memory theory made "the inquiry concerning a future life of no consequence at all to us, the persons who are making it" (Butler 1736, 99). By "a future life," Butler meant specifically to be talking about the possibility of resurrection. Developing this point, Swinburne argues that, on a reductionist theory:

> for me to hope for my resurrection is for me to hope for the future existence of a man with my memories and character, that is, a man who will be able to remember the things which happened to me and react to circumstances somewhat as I do. But that's not at all what I hope for in hoping for my resurrection. I don't hope that *there be* a man of that kind – I want it to be me. If it isn't to be me, then despite my hope for my resurrection, I am probably relatively indifferent to whether or not a man rises with my character and memories. And if I

am to rise again, I probably shouldn't mind *all* that much if
I had lost many of my memories and much of my bad character. What matters is that *I* rise. (Swinburne 1973–4, 244)

Although Butler and Swinburne specifically address our egoistic concern with respect to resurrection, the point generalizes. Suppose, for example, that I learn that someone will be
in pain tomorrow. As argued by Madell, though it is obvious
that I have reason for egoistic concern if the person who will
be in pain is me, "it is not at all obvious that I have *any*
reason to be concerned about the fact that the person who
will be in pain will have a certain set of memory impressions"
(Madell 1981, 110). On his view, the failure of reductionist
theories to justify our special concern constitutes an "abso-
lutely central objection" to such theories (1981, 109).

Reductionists have responded to these criticisms in a
variety of ways. With respect to our egoistic concern, some
have simply bitten the bullet. Parfit, for example, accepts that
it may well be true that, on a reductionist view, we have *no
reason at all to be concerned about our own futures*. That
said, he also tries to show that psychological continuity and
connectedness may give us some reason for concern even if
there is no further fact. Others dispute that the further fact
view does any better at justifying our egoistic concern than
the reductionist view.

As for the criticism that only the further fact view is compatible with identity in the strict and philosophical sense,
reductionists might model their response on the sorts of considerations invoked by the four-dimensionalist. A tree has
many spatial parts, not all of which have exactly the same
properties. The tree's leaves are green and smooth while its
trunk is brown and rough. But despite this variation among
its spatial parts, the tree as a spatial whole is a single thing,
strictly identical to itself. Likewise, the fact that the tree has
some variation among its temporal parts – that it has green
leaves in May and orange and red leaves in October – does
not mean that the tree as a temporal whole is not a single
thing, strictly identical to itself. And we can say something
similar about persons as well.

The criticisms aimed at the psychological and physical
theories launched by proponents of the further fact view thus

do not seem to be decisive. Moreover, the further fact view itself faces significant criticism. First, we saw in chapter 2 that Locke denies that sameness of souls is sufficient to constitute personal identity. Even if some present-day person happened to have the same non-physical soul as Thersites, we would be disinclined to accept that he could be identical to Thersites unless he also has experiential memories of Thersites' life. Second, and even more fundamentally, various worries have been raised about the very coherence of the idea of non-physical souls. We might wonder, for example, how non-physical entities could be distinguished from one another. In the absence of any matter to distinguish them, what could possibly make your non-physical soul a different thing from my non-physical soul? Moreover, since a non-physical soul is supposed to be unchanging – otherwise it could not account for identity in the strict and philosophical sense – we cannot rely on psychological properties to distinguish it from other non-physical souls. Psychological properties, after all, undergo change over time.

Of course, if we had independent evidence for the existence of non-physical souls, such evidence would undermine the charge of incoherence and thereby provide some measure of support for the further fact view. Importantly, religious teachings cannot count as the relevant kind of evidence. Things we take on faith we believe independently of reasons. But suppose, for example, that we had some kind of empirical confirmation of people's "near-death experiences," i.e., suppose we verified that such individuals survived after the physical death of their bodies. Alternatively, suppose we had evidence for the occurrence of reincarnation. To borrow an example from Parfit, suppose that a 21st-century woman seems to have memories of life as a Celtic hunter in the Bronze Age. And suppose that she made various claims that are verified by archaeologists. In a spot that has been undisturbed for at least two millennia, for example, they might find a bracelet that she claims to have buried during her former lifetime. Since there is no way that this 21st-century woman could have the same brain, or any other physical continuity with a Bronze Age hunter, it might start to seem that the only way to explain the case is by positing some sort of non-physical soul that had once been associated with the

Bronze Age hunter and is now associated with this 21st-century woman. Evidence of this sort would certainly support the further fact view. Unfortunately, however, there does not seem to be any such evidence. As natural as it may be to look for some other view when we become frustrated with the limitations of the psychological and physical theories, the further fact view does not seem to be the magic answer.

5.2   Hybrid Views

But perhaps there is another possibility. Instead of looking for a completely different alternative to the psychological and physical theories, perhaps instead we should look for some way to combine them. Williams, for example, has argued that certain psychological facts are inextricably bound up with physical facts. Suppose we performed a procedure like The Swap discussed in chapter 4 on an emperor and a peasant who are vastly different physically. In such a procedure, each individual has his or her psychology downloaded from his or her brain, temporarily placed in a storage device, and then re-uploaded to the other individual's brain, so the emperor's psychology is now in the peasant's body and the peasant's psychology is in the emperor's body. Since voices are functions of the physical bodies involved, the peasant's psychology must now be verbally expressed in the emperor's voice, and vice versa. But, as Williams worries, the peasant's "gruff blasphemies" might simply be unutterable in the emperor's cultivated voice. The emperor might have a face that's not at all suited to expressing the peasant's characteristic look of morose suspiciousness, while the peasant might have a face that's equally unsuited to expressing the emperor's "fastidious arrogance." Absent the ability to smile his characteristic smile, would the emperor's personality still be the same (Williams 1956–7, 12)? Relatedly, American philosopher Susan Brison has argued that memory is essentially embodied. By attending specifically to the case of traumatic memory, Brison suggests that it may not be as simple as we might have thought to develop a memory theory in isolation of bodily considerations (Brison 2002, 44–5). In the face of issues like this, conjoined with the difficulties facing both psychological and physical theories, it would be natural to consider whether we could develop a hybrid view that would achieve the best of both worlds.

As tempting as this suggestion is, however, there's good reason to think that it is unlikely to be successful. The problem is perhaps best seen schematically. Any hybrid view has to be either *conjunctive* or *disjunctive* in nature. Conjunctive views will require a combination of *both* psychological and biological continuity for personal identity over time, while disjunctive views will require *either* psychological or biological continuity for personal identity over time. Unfortunately, both kinds of hybrid view thus inherit the problems of the original views themselves.

First, let's consider conjunctive views. Depending on what kind of physical continuity is required, such views may be able to accommodate the transplant intuition. If, for example, the physical continuity required is brain continuity, then the individual who receives your brain will indeed be you. But the conjunctive view cannot accommodate our intuitions in either the upload case or the teleportation case. If both psychological and physical continuity are required, then transporting and uploading are equivalent to death, since in neither case is any physical continuity preserved. Moreover, the fact that the view requires psychological continuity implies that you were never a fetus.

Disjunctive views initially seem to fare much better. Since all that is required is that there be *either* psychological continuity or biological continuity, then it will be true that you were once a fetus (since there is physical continuity between the fetus that was once in your mother's womb and you), and you will be able to survive both uploading and teleportation (since there is psychological continuity between you and the uploaded and transported individuals). Moreover, if the relevant kind of physical continuity is brain continuity, then disjunctive views will also be able to handle the transplant case. But now let's go back once again to The Swap. Recall Aaron and Baron, who participated in such a procedure in chapter 4. After The Swap, the individual we'd called A.Bod (because he has Aaron's body) has Aaron's brain, but the individual we'd called B.Bod (because he has Baron's body) has Aaron's psychology. Aaron is thus physically but not psychologically continuous with A.Bod, and psychologically but not physically continuous with B.Bod. Yet since the disjunctive hybrid view requires only one kind of continuity to be present, it looks like Aaron is identical to both A.Bod *and* B.Bod, violating transitivity of identity. To make matters worse, it looks like Baron is also identical to both A.Bod and B.Bod (he shares psychological continuity with A.Bod and physical continuity with B.Bod). Such a result is clearly unacceptable. As this suggests, the disjunctive hybrid view faces both logical trouble and a problem of reduplication even more severe than the one faced by the psychological view itself.

Granted, the versions of hybrid views we've considered are very crude ones. Perhaps there could be more sophisticated hybrid theories that avoid some of these issues. For example, in her most recent work the American philosopher Marya Schechtman has argued for a theory she calls *the person life view*. Underlying the view is Schechtman's suspicion that "what actually constitutes the continuation of a person is not some one of the relations found in the tangle of intertwined connections present in paradigmatic cases of personal identity, but rather the tangle itself" (Schechtman 2014, 201). On the person life view, persons are defined in terms of the kinds of characteristic lives they lead; to be a person is to be an entity living a "person life." There are three general elements that make up a person life: (1) individual capacities, both psychological and biological, some of which may be missing or which may become lost or attenuated over time; (2) typical activities and interactions such as interpersonal relationships; and (3) a social/cultural infrastructure. This "property cluster" conception of a person life gives rise to a theory of personal identity over time: a person's identity over time consists in the continuation of a person life. In saying this, Schechtman explicitly refrains from giving necessary and sufficient conditions for personal identity over time. One cannot give such conditions, she argues, because there are none. Rather:

> Instead of assuming some one of the relations present in paradigmatic cases of continuation is the one that constitutes our

identity, we can think instead of identity as constituted by their interactions with one another. On the standard approach [such as a psychological or physical theory] the fact that biological, psychological, and social continuities are intertwined is seen as a complication which makes it difficult to determine which relation constitutes continuation. On the property cluster model the integrated functioning *is* the true nature of the relation that constitutes the conditions of our continuation. (Schechtman 2014, 150)

It's not clear, however, that the person life view really offers us a theory of personal identity over time. Rather, it simply shifts the burden to developing a theory of person life. When a person's psychology is uploaded to a computer, does that count as a continuation of the person life? When a person's brain is transplanted into a new body, does that count as a continuation of the same person life? In answering these questions, Schechtman ends up relying heavily on facts about how we would treat the individual in such a case. On her view, facts about personal identity are at least partly dependent on social norms and conventions. (For other conventionalist views, see Johnston 1989 and Unger 1990.) But it is hard to see how the question of personal identity – the metaphysical question of whether some future person is me – could depend on such norms. It seems conceptually possible, for example, that societal norms could be wrong – that there could be cases in which society does not recognize me as having survived even though I actually did. For this reason, even if a principled and plausible conception of the notion of person life could be developed, the adoption of this sort of view seems to come at considerable cost.

Ultimately, then, hybrid views do not seem to hold much promise. Though the psychological theory and the physical theory both have problems, these problems cannot be avoided simply through some sort of combined approach. Rather, we must face up to the problems more directly. But perhaps this conclusion is too hasty. As we noted at the beginning of this chapter, there are two different reactions that one might have to the difficulties that confront the psychological and physical theories. We have so far been discussing the first such reaction – that there is some better alternative lurking out there – and we have seen why such an alternative is unlikely to be found.

But what about the second reaction? Might it be the case that there is simply no answer to the question of personal identity?

Interestingly, the same line of reasoning that helps us to see the shortcomings of the first reaction helps us also to see the shortcomings of the second reaction. As have just noted, it seems conceptually possible that societal judgments about an individual's personal identity over time could be wrong. But the sense that there could be a wrong answer about these questions entails that there's a right answer to these questions. Such an answer might be out of our grasp – we might not know what it is, we might not be able at present to correctly formulate a theory of personal identity over time – but there must be an answer. There must be some fact of the matter in which personal identity consists.

Importantly, saying this does not itself amount to a rejection of the "Identity Doesn't Matter" view we discussed in chapter 3. That view, associated with the work of Derek Parfit, claims that there might be some cases in which questions of personal identity lack an answer, that there might be some cases in which our identity is indeterminate. But the fact that there are borderline cases does not mean that there is no correct theory of personal identity. There are borderline cases of what counts as a heap, or what counts as being bald, but that does not mean that the notions of heap and baldness cannot be given an analysis. Moreover, recall that Parfit himself gives a theory of personal identity, one according to which personal identity consists in non-branching psychological continuity and connectedness. Thus, the reaction that we are now considering – that there might be no answer to the reidentification question – is considerably more radical than the view advocated by Parfit.

Drawing out some of the implications of this second reaction helps us to see exactly how radical it is. Today, after I finish work, I will go to pick up my sons from school. According to the reaction that we're now considering, however, there is no fact of the matter about whether the two children I pick up are the same children I dropped off this morning. In fact, there is no fact of the matter about whether I was really the one to drop them off. There is no fact of the matter about whether the person I married 15 years ago is the same person who will walk in the door this evening after having taken the train home from work. There is no fact of the matter as to whether the individual who is now governing in Washington, DC, is the same person as the one who was elected in the last US presidential election. Considered in this light, the reaction we're now considering seems not only radical, but downright crazy. As difficult as the question of reidentification may be, the difficulty itself cannot justify us in believing that there is no answer.

5.3   What Are We looking For From a Theory of Personal Identity?

At this point, however, there is a third reaction that might also be natural. Perhaps the difficulty in resolving the reidentification question comes from an overly high set of expectations. At various points in our discussion, we have seen that our pretheoretic intuitions about personal identity often pull us in different directions. On the one hand, we think we were once fetuses, but on the other hand, we think we could survive the destruction of our biological organism. On the one hand, we think that teleportation is a means of travel, but on the other hand, we are wary about treating reduplication as a case of double survival. Schechtman's sense that there is a tangle here is undoubtedly correct. Perhaps, then, it is too much to expect that a theory of personal identity is going to unsnarl the knots. Moreover, if our intuitions are not just tangled but actually inconsistent, then it would simply be impossible for any theory of personal identity to account for them all.

Underlying our discussion of personal identity has been what philosopher Carsten Korfmacher (2006) has called the *Big Assumption* – namely, that an adequate theory of personal identity must accept all of our intuitive judgments about the various cases and thought experiments that we've been considering. But it now seems likely that the Big Assumption is mistaken. Once we accept that no theory of personal identity will be able to accommodate all of our pretheoretic intuitions, we will correspondingly need to lower our expectations in assessing the different theories. The questions facing us now become: What are the relevant strengths of our competing intuitions? Which ones can be most easily explained away or reinterpreted to have different implications from those we originally identified? Which ones are simply bedrock, unshakable and immune to revision or reinterpretation?

In lowering our expectations, we should also consider more directly what we want from a theory of personal identity. Here it will be helpful to consider some of Schechtman's earlier work (work prior to her development of the person life view). In her important book *The Constitution of Selves* (1996), Schechtman suggests that we need to reorient discussions of personal identity by separating two questions of personal identity: the reidentification question that we have been considering over the course of the last four chapters, and a different question that she calls *the characterization question*. While the reidentification question asks what it is for a person to be the same person over time, the characterization question asks what makes us who we really are. According to Schechtman, conflation of the reidentification question and the characterization question puts undue pressure on theories of reidentification. When we fail to recognize the multifaceted nature of issues of personal identity, we expect theories of reidentification to elucidate matters that they are ill suited to address. This general line of argument is also frequently associated with the twentieth-century French philosopher Paul Ricoeur; on his view, the failure to distinguish between two senses of identity – identity as *sameness* and identity as *self* – has been largely responsible for many of the difficulties which obscure the question of personal identity (Ricoeur 1991, 73).

In her own development of this argument, Schechtman asks us to consider various practical concerns that seem intermixed with our thinking about personal identity. As she notes, "It is a fundamental feature of persons that facts about their identities have deeply significant practical implications" (Schechtman 1996, 14). Of the many practical matters that have deep-seated connections to theories of personal identity, Schechtman focuses on four that she takes to be particularly important:

- survival
- egoistic concern
- moral responsibility
- compensatory fairness.

(handwritten:) practical matters
imp for person identy
" four features

The first two are familiar to us already. The third, moral responsibility, <u>concerns an individual's accountability for her</u> own actions. Importantly, moral responsibility comes apart from <u>legal</u> responsibility. Someone may be morally responsible for all kinds of things – insulting a colleague, ignoring a student's email, failing to speak up in the face of injustice or to make adequate charitable contributions – for which she bears no legal responsibility. Legal prohibitions simply do not extend to these sorts of matters. Schechtman's fourth item, compensatory fairness, <u>concerns the balance between burdens</u> and benefits: when is a present burden appropriately compensated by some future benefit (or vice versa)? Consider the pain of a vaccination shot versus its protection against disease, or the difficulty of saving money versus being able to live comfortably in retirement.

Following Schechtman, we will simply call these the *four features*. In each case, the relation to personal identity looks to be straightforward. First, and perhaps most fundamentally, theories of personal identity should explain when and in what circumstances we survive in the future. When is it rational for me to think of some future experience as mine, for me to *anticipate* it? The link between personal identity and survival is one that has already come up at several points in our discussion. Second, as we noted in our discussion of the further fact view, theories of personal identity can be reasonably expected to make sense of the rationality of our egoistic concern. Third, since it seems reasonable that a person can be held accountable only for her own actions, it seems that theories of personal identity are relevant to determining the facts of moral responsibility. Finally, facts about personal identity also seem relevant to the question of when an imposed burden will be fairly compensated by some future benefit. Parents can burden their child with the pain of a vaccination shot since the child will be the one to reap the future benefit of protection from disease. More generally, it seems, a person is compensated for some present burden only if she is the one to experience the future benefit. The link to personal identity is thus obvious.

But, however obvious the link between these four features and personal identity in general, Schechtman argues that it is considerably less obvious that such features should be linked to the reidentification question in particular. To see this, it may be helpful to return to one of the cases we have previously encountered, that of distant transporter malfunction. Recall Margaret O'Malley, who is about to teleport to New York to see her dying father. Because of a transporter malfunction, Meg materializes in New York while Peg materializes in New Zealand; then, several minutes after arrival, a freak accident at the New Zealand transporter station leads to Peg's annihilation. Margaret is not identical to either Meg or Peg, since identity is a relation that holds one-to-one and not one-to-many. Peg's death, when it occurs, does not change the facts about numerical identity. Meg is still not numerically identical to Margaret. How does this lack of numerical identity affect our thinking about the four features? For example, what's the relation between Margaret's moral responsibilities and Meg's moral responsibilities? Suppose that Margaret had promised her father that she'd come to see him as soon as she arrived in New York. Does Meg have a moral obligation to keep this promise, or did any such obligation die with Margaret? Likewise, suppose that Margaret caused a minor traffic accident while rushing to get to the transporter station in central London. Should Meg have to pay for the damages, or does the fact that she is not numerically identical to Margaret absolve her of any responsibility in the matter? Considering such a case, I expect most of us will think that Meg inherits Margaret's moral responsibilities. She must go visit Mr. O'Malley, "her" father, and she must pay for the damage caused in the fender bender. Even though she is not numerically identical to Margaret, the facts about *who she is* nonetheless support this conclusion. It's precisely these sorts of facts that are relevant to the characterization question.

In a discussion influenced by Schechtman, David Shoemaker nicely generalizes this line of reasoning:

> In seeking to account for anticipation, we seem to be wondering, "What makes those expected future experiences *mine*?"

> In seeking to account for self-concern, we seem to be wondering, "What makes those future states I'm specially concerned about *mine*?" And similarly with questions of responsibility and compensation: "What makes those actions for which I'm responsible – or those burdens for which I'm to be compensated – *mine*?" (Shoemaker 2009, 90)

Given that none of these questions as stated makes any reference to issues of reidentification, we can see why the expectation that theories of reidentification will answer them might be unreasonable.

On Schechtman's view – or at least, on the view she develops in *The Constitution of Selves* – this unreasonable expectation has led us improperly to discount physical theories of reidentification. The push/pull of intuitions about psychological continuity vs. physical continuity in the sorts of cases we've been considering arises not because the psychological theory and physical theory are competing answers to a single question but because they are distinct answers to distinct questions. While psychological facts are indeed relevant to personal identity, they are relevant only to the characterization question. In contrast, physical facts are the facts relevant to the reidentification question. David DeGrazia, another philosopher who attends carefully to the separation of the reidentification question and the characterization question, has argued along similar lines. Though he endorses animalism, claiming that our numerical identity over time consists in biological continuity, he makes room for our intuitions about the importance of psychological continuity by arguing that it plays a critical role in answering the characterization question (DeGrazia 2005).

Let's call the general strategy endorsed by Schechtman and DeGrazia the *divide-and-conquer strategy*. This strategy certainly leads to a tidy solution to the messy problem of personal identity that we've been considering. Recall once more the transplant case: suppose that your brain is about to be transplanted into another body. The divide-and-conquer strategy suggests that, though it would be a mistake to think that the resulting individual would be numerically identical to you, the pull that we feel toward saying this can be explained in terms of facts about characterization. Despite the lack of numerical identity, it could be appropriate for you to anticipate the experiences of that resulting individual. It could be appropriate for such an individual to be held morally responsible for your actions now. Burdens that you've previously undertaken could be fairly compensated by benefits to that individual. You could have what matters in survival, even though the resulting individual would not be numerically identical to you.

In this way, the divide-and-conquer strategy reinterpets the intuitions that seemed to pull us in favor of a psychological theory of reidentification: understood correctly, such intuitions really show the important role that psychological facts play in characterization. But it is not clear that our intuitions can be explained away this easily. When I think of the future individual who has my brain, I'm inclined to think, "That's me," not just, "That's someone who for all intents and purposes you can treat as me." I don't think of that person as someone who can seamlessly substitute as mother to my children. I think of it as a case where *I* continue to mother my children.

That said, attempting to unsnarl our tangle of intuitions is a tricky matter, and we cannot hope to do it fully here. But perhaps a better way to see the problem with the conclusion drawn by Schechtman and DeGrazia after employing the divide-and-conquer strategy is to explore how such a strategy might just as well have been used to support the opposite conclusion. Consider the fetus problem. Proponents of animalism argue, plausibly, that psychological continuity theorists are committed to the claim that none of us was ever a fetus. Though such a claim seems implausible, the divide – and-conquer strategy here proves useful. Though you are not numerically identical to the fetus that was once in your mother's womb, burdens imposed on that fetus can be appropriately compensated by future benefits to you. For example, fetal surgery can now be performed to correct a number of congenital birth defects such as spina bifida. Though such a surgery is hard on the fetus, that hardship is offset by the benefits accrued to the person who is born. Here the psychological facts seem relevant to numerical identity, while the biological facts seem relevant to compensatory fairness and hence to questions of characterization.

Thus, though we will follow Schechtman and DeGrazia in separating the reidentification question and the characterization question, our doing so should not be seen as an endorsement of the divide-and-conquer strategy or the particular conclusion that they've drawn from it. We will not be assuming that facts about psychological continuity are irrelevant to questions of reidentification. And more generally, we will not be assuming that facts about reidentification are irrelevant to the four features. (This latter point is one with which Schechtman and DeGrazia would undoubtedly agree.) Rather, in separating the characterization question from the reidentification question, what we will be assuming is that facts about reidentification are not the only facts relevant to the four features. There are other facts about personal identity – facts best considered under the rubric of the characterization question – that are relevant as well.

Though our discussion in this section has doused the hope that we can untie the tangled knot of intuitions with which we've been grappling simply by introducing this third question of personal identity to go alongside the questions of identification and reidentification, its introduction should nonetheless ease the burden on theories of reidentification. The dissatisfaction that we feel when grappling with theories of reidentification may well arise at least in part from the failure adequately to attend to the issue of characterization in addition to the issue of reidentification. Until now, we have been relying on theories of reidentification to do all the work related to issues of personal identity. It is thus time – if not past time – to turn our attention directly to the characterization question.

5.4 The Characterization Question

Individuals have all sorts of characteristics – from passions to phobias, from habits to hang-ups. Some of our characteristics, however, seem more central to our identities than others. The characterization question focuses on this issue. As introduced by Schechtman, the characterization question asks what it means to say that a particular characteristic is really a characteristic of a given person, i.e., which are the characteristics that go toward making her who she is. In a sense, then, the characterization question presents us with another question about identification rather than reidentification. As should be clear, however, it is not the question of what makes something a person but rather the question of what makes a particular person the person that she is.

Questions about characterization are familiar from fiction and film. When Luke Skywalker battles Darth Vader on the Death Star, he feels a conflict between the goodness within him and the allure of the Dark Side. When Harry Potter experiences Voldemort's thoughts and desires because of the connection between their minds, he struggles not to incorporate Voldmort's desires as his own. When Aang searches for a way to defeat Fire Lord Ozai, he's torn between his duties as Avatar and his own deep-seated aversion to killing. In each of these cases, versions of the characterization question arise. Is there really a core of darkness deep within Luke? Is the desire to go to the Ministry of Magic really Harry's own? Would killing Fire Lord Ozai go against Aang's very nature?

These fictional depictions mirror the questions about characterization that often arise in everyday life. They are perhaps particularly prominent when someone is in the midst of major life events. As college students face college graduation, the impending transition from being a student to heading out into the real world often leads them to question who they really are. Some students grapple with a complete lack of direction, as when someone simply doesn't know what she wants to do with her future. Other students grapple with having too many potential directions, as when someone feels deeply conflicted between her desire to make a high salary and pay off her student loan debts and her competing desire to make a real difference in the world. We might think also of people grappling with questions about their sexuality, or coping with the aftermath of a seriously traumatic incident. Whether such situations lead to introspective self-reflection or to a full-blown "identity crisis," what's at issue are precisely the kinds of concerns that underlie the characterization question.

Although the characterization question came to particular prominence in discussions of personal identity because of Schechtman's work, it has long been discussed by philosophers

– often in the context of ethics and moral psychology. As Schechtman herself notes, Harry Frankfurt (whose theory of personhood we encountered earlier in chapter 1) gave a particularly insightful expression of the relevant issues:

> We think it correct to attribute to a person, in the strict sense, only some of the events in the history of his body. The others – those with respect to which he is passive – have their moving principles outside of him, and we do not identify him with these events. Certain events in the history of a person's mind, likewise, have their moving principles outside of him. He is passive with respect to them, and they are likewise not to be attributed to him. A person is no more to be identified with everything that goes on in his mind, in other words, than he is to be identified with everything that goes on in his body. (Frankfurt 1976, 242–3)

An answer to the characterization question would help us to distinguish between those characteristics with respect to which we are merely passive and those characteristics with respect to which we are not. It is only the latter that belong to the set of characteristics that make a person who she truly is. The terminology of *identification* used in this passage often surfaces in discussions of characterization. Not all of a person's characteristics are ones with which she identifies, and thus not all of them are ones that can be genuinely attributable to her.

To see how a shift from the reidentification question to the characterization question is helpful in making progress on certain questions of personal identity, consider the famous case involving the kidnapping of Patty Hearst. The granddaughter of newspaper tycoon William Randolph Hearst, Patty was kidnapped in 1974 at the age of 19 by the Symbionese Liberation Army (SLA). The SLA were a left-wing terrorist revolutionary group. Among other things, their members were responsible for the 1973 murder of Oakland school superintendent Marcus Foster. After being held captive by the SLA for almost two months, Patty decided to join them and claimed to be fully committed to their goals. She adopted the name "Tania" and subsequently took part in an armed bank robbery in San Francisco. Though photographs of the robbery suggest that she was not being coerced to take part, and though she refused to give evidence against the captured SLA members, her defense team at trial argued that she had been systematically brainwashed by her captors after her kidnapping. After allegedly blindfolding her, imprisoning her in a small closet, and subjecting her to both physical and sexual abuse, her captors used a form of mind control that succeeded in breaking her. Patty was ultimately arrested and convicted of bank robbery. Initially sentenced to 35 years, she later had her sentence commuted by President Jimmy Carter and ended up serving less than 2 years. In 2001, she received a pardon from President Bill Clinton in one of his final acts in office.

Was Patty really responsible for her actions while she was kidnapped? Issues of personal identity seem clearly to be intertwined in sorting out the answer to this question, but it is not clear that the issues are ones of reidentification. We are not primarily interested in whether the person who committed the robbery was numerically the same person as Patty Hearst, either before or after her kidnapping. On either of the two competing theories of reidentification, this question would be answered in the affirmative. Clearly there was no break of physical continuity, and while the brainwashing caused psychological disruption, it did not sever the kidnap victim's psychological continuity with her past self (she retained all her memories, for example). Rather, what seems to matter here are issues of characterization: were the actions undertaken *truly hers*?

At this point, however, skepticism might arise. When we try to determine what it could mean for some actions to be truly attributable to the person who stands before us, it might seem that we are simply asking whether the relevant action was committed by the person who stands before us – whether they are numerically identical to the one who acted. So, despite the different phrasing, we seem nonetheless to be right back to the reidentification question. Might the characterization question thus simply be a variant of the reidentification question?

Explicitly addressing this kind of worry, Schechtman grants that the two questions are closely related – so closely related, in fact, that one may simply seem to be a rephrasing of the other. But, while she also explicitly grants that rephrasing a question cannot make a difference to the facts about the world, she astutely notes that the way that we phrase a question can obscure certain facts or render them inexpressible (Schechtman 1996, 91). To see this point, just think about how facts get lost by the phrasing of questions in political debates, as when one candidate asks another, "Was it your support for terrorism that prevented you from voting to send troops to Afghanistan?" Or think about what happens in the phenomenon of push polling, as when a pollster asks a prospective voter, "If you knew that Mayor Jones was being investigated for corruption, would you be more or less likely to vote for her reelection?" Even if allegations of corruption have never been raised against Mayor Jones, the question certainly leaves the impression that an investigation is occurring and plants suspicion in the mind of the voter.

To help us see the distinction between the two questions, Schechtman emphasizes that the respect in which they differ is their *logical form*. When we ask the reidentification question, we are focused on the relation between two distinct person-stages that will make them stages of the same person. When we ask the characterization question, we are focused on the relation between a person and particular characteristics that are hers. The relata – the things being related to one another – are different in each case, and so, as Schechtman says, the form of the relation itself will be different. In her view, this variation in logical form is a "difference that makes a difference" (Schechtman 1996, 77–8).

In the final chapter of this book, we will thus turn to issues of characterization. In doing so, we leave unresolved how best to sort out the conflicting intuitions that we have been confronted with in our discussion of the reidentification question. Some of the issues may well become clearer in coming years as technologies advance. If – or, as some would say, *when* – we come face to face with an android body that contains the uploaded consciousness of a dear friend, or when we confront the decision whether to use a transporter, this will likely help us to sharpen our intuitions about whether such cases maintain personal identity. In the meantime, however, the debate between the psychological approach and the physical approach will undoubtedly continue.

Further Reading

A useful discussion of the strict and philosophical sense of identity can be found in Chisholm (1977). For historical defenses of the further fact view, a good place to begin is with the texts by Butler and Reid excerpted in Perry's (2008) anthology. For contemporary defenses of this view, see Swinburne (1973–4) and Madell (1981); Baker (2007, 2012) offers a version of the view that is compatible with our being essentially embodied.

Parfit's discussion of whether our egoistic concern can be justified if a reductionist view of personal identity is true comes primarily in chapter 14 of *Reasons and Persons* (Parfit 1984). Perry explores how such concern might be justified in Perry (1976).

Schechtman (1996) discusses the characterization question in detail. Shoemaker (2009, ch. 3) also contains a helpful discussion of this question and how it is to be distinguished from the reidentification question.

6
Narrative Identity

As we have seen, philosophical discussion of the reidentification question takes place within the context of a debate among three competing alternatives: the psychological approach, the physical approach, and the non-reductionist (further fact) approach. In contrast, the debate about characterization does not feature fundamentally different approaches but has instead tended to focus heavily on a single theoretical framework, that of narrativity. On this general approach, the characteristics that constitute an individual's identity – the characteristics that make a person the person that she is – are those that cohere together in a narrative structure. An individual's identity in the sense relevant to the characterization question derives from the role she plays as the central character in the story of her life.

Philosophers are not alone in looking to narrativity when attempting to understand personal identity. We find similar explorations in psychology, psychoanalysis, sociology, theology, literary studies, and a variety of other disciplines. More generally, the quest for narrative structure in our lives, and our tendency to treat our lives as unfolding stories, surfaces as a recurrent theme throughout popular culture. There are at least seven distinct songs with the title "Story of My Life" (and two more if you add in a "The" at the start), recorded by a diverse collection of artists such as the country-and-western singer Marty Robbins, the pop punk group Social Distortion, and the British boy band One Direction.

Yass!

In philosophical discussion of the characterization question, the focus on narrativity has been so single-minded that it is hard even to see what kinds of alternative approaches there might be for answering the characterization question. In fact, rather than contrasting the narrative approach with alternate approaches to characterization, its proponents tend to frame their discussion as a contrast between two types of identity: narrative identity and numerical identity. (This is not to say that the narrative theory is taken to *compete* with theories of numerical identity. As we saw in the previous chapter, such theories might be complementary to one another insofar as each is relevant to different kinds of concerns.) When it comes to the characterization question, the narrative theory is more or less the only game in town.

Despite the absence of alternative theories of characterization, however, there have nonetheless been important criticisms of the narrative approach. Some have worried that we lack an adequate understanding of the very notion of narrativity. Others have argued that it is a mistake to assign narrativity an essential role in constituting our identity as persons. But before we can get to these criticisms, we need to develop a better understanding of the narrative theory.

In fact, it is something of a mistake to refer to *the* narrative theory of personal identity, because there are really two distinct types of theories on offer in the philosophical literature that go under this same heading. In chapter 1, in focusing our attention on metaphysical personhood, we distinguished it from the closely related notion of moral personhood. As we saw, while metaphysical personhood is a descriptive notion, moral personhood is a normative or prescriptive notion. A similar distinction needs to be drawn when considering theories of narrative identity. Descriptive versions of such theories tell us that conceiving of one's life in terms of a narrative structure plays an essential role in constituting one's identity as a person. In contrast, prescriptive versions of such theories tell us that we *should* conceive of our lives in terms of a narrative structure, that doing so plays an essential role in the pursuit of an ethically good life. American philosopher Charles Taylor has been particularly influential in developing a theory of the latter sort. On his view, understanding our lives in narrative form is an essential part of our attempt to orient ourselves toward goodness (Taylor 1989, see especially 47–52). In discussions of narrativity in the philosophical literature, these two sorts of theories are often developed in conjunction with one another, and they are thus not always as carefully distinguished as one might want. However, in what follows – in line with our general orientation toward metaphysical inquiry – we will focus on descriptive versions of the narrative theory of identity.

6.1 Narrative Structure

The notion of narrativity plays an important role in narrative theories of identity. Central to such theories is the claim that an individual's identity emerges from the integration of events and characteristics into a narrative structure. But what does it mean for something to have narrative structure?

Suppose you missed last night's baseball game, and you want to find out what happened. When you open the morning newspaper or go to the ESPN website, you might just check the box score, or you might read a reporter's account of the game. Although both convey information to you, they do so differently. Unlike the box score, the reporter's account presents you with a narrative – it brings the events of the game together in a connected fashion. The box score provides an extensive array of information, and it undoubtedly contains lots of interesting facts and statistics that are not included in the reporter's account. But though you might be able to extract a story from the facts and statistics presented in the box score, the box score itself does not tell you that story; it does not take narrative form. Box scores, like shopping lists and weather forecasts, convey information in a non-narrative way.

Just as information about baseball games can be conveyed both narratively and non-narratively, so too can information about persons. After an annual physical with your physician, you might get a printout summarizing your vital statistics: age, height, weight, blood pressure, and so on. Though the printout contains a vast amount of information about you, that information is not organized in a narrative way. But now, suppose the physician were to dictate notes to your file after the visit: "Patient, age 21, reports that after her annual physical last year, she began an exercise program. She has lost 15 pounds in the last year, and she has also lowered both her blood pressure and her cholesterol levels." These dictated notes, though they present much of the same information as the summary printout, bring the facts together in such a way that the account starts to take on a narrative structure.

Both the reporter's story and the physician's notes are examples of nonfictional narratives, but narratives can of course also be works of fiction. When it comes to fictional narratives, it would be misleading to talk about facts being conveyed as we did with nonfictional narratives. Given that Nancy Drew does not exist, the books in which she's featured do not provide us with factual information about actual investigations that have been conducted by an actual teenage sleuth. But what matters for narrativity is the way that the events of the story are presented and not whether they have really occurred.

In an interesting discussion and development of the narrative theory, American philosopher Hilde Lindemann has usefully distinguished four different features required for something to have narrative structure (Lindemann 2001, 11–15). First, a narrative is *depictive*. Importantly, however, not all depictions are narrative in structure. Rather, a narrative is a depiction of a certain sort. When you visit the Taj Mahal and take a selfie in front of it, that photograph depicts you, but because it captures you only at a single moment of time, it lacks narrative structure. Narratives must be *dynamic* rather than *static* depictions. They must depict a series of events that take place over time.

How such events are depicted can vary considerably from narrative to narrative. Unlike a mere chronicle of events, which must follow a strict chronological sequence, the order in which a narrative depicts a series of events need not correspond directly to the temporal order in which the events occurred. The reporter's account of last night's baseball game, for example, might begin with the game-winning hit in the ninth inning. More generally, movies and novels that are narrative in structure often utilize both flashbacks and flash-forwards. To give just one particularly vivid example, Christopher Nolan's film *Memento* implements an unusual and complex reverse temporal structure to depict the events that occur to its central character Leonard, a man suffering from anterograde amnesia.

Second, in depicting a series of events, a narrative is *selective* in that it need not be a wholly comprehensive rendering of everything that has ever occurred to the subject of the narrative. *42*, the 2013 biographical film about Jackie Robinson, the first African-American player in Major League Baseball, depicts only some of the incidents of racism he encountered. Likewise, in reporting on last night's baseball game, the journalist need not include a description of the events of every inning, let alone a description of every pitch thrown.

Third, a narrative is *interpretive*. The interpretation it offers comes through the characterization of characters, events, and places. Sometimes the interpretation proceeds explicitly, as when the Stage Manager in Thornton Wilder's *Our Town* serves not as a neutral narrator but rather as someone who deliberately shapes our understanding of what's happening in Grover's Corners. Other times, the interpretative overlay proceeds more implicitly. The change from black-and-white to color upon Dorothy's arrival in Oz affects one's interpretation of *The Wizard of Oz*, and in general a film's lighting and score influence a viewer's sense of the events that are unfolding.

Fourth, a narrative is *connective*. Events are connected with other events and also with other interconnected features of the narrative such as setting, tone, and character. While this connectivity can take many forms, perhaps the most central form of narrative connectivity is causal in nature. When an account has narrative structure, events are linked not just temporally but causally. It's also worth noting that narratives are often connected to other narratives via characters, themes, or even plots. The Broadway musical *Rent* loosely reimagines the story of Puccini's opera *La Bohème* as set in late twentieth-century New York. Sports reporting often casts a team's success as a "Cinderella story." And well before *The Avengers* was released in theaters, cameo appearances by Samuel Jackson as Agent Nick Fury connected films like *Iron Man, Captain America,* and *Thor.*

These four different aspects of narratives delineated by Lindemann are themselves connected to one another. Which events are selected for inclusion helps to shape the interpretation of a story, while the ways in which events are causally connected to one another help to shape which events are selected for inclusion. Ultimately, it's the interplay of these four different aspects of narratives that enables a narrative to develop thematically. It's also what enables a narrative to express some sort of meaning. This too helps differentiate narratives from non-narratives like shopping lists, selfies, and mere chronicles. As Lindemann colorfully notes, "A chronicle is just one damned thing after another, whereas a story embodies an understanding" (Lindemann 2001, 15). Similarly, the fact that the individual events depicted by a narrative "take their meaning from the broader context of the story in which they occur" is what Schechtman points to as the most salient feature of the narrative form (Schechtman 1996, 96). This last point – the fact that a narrative embodies understanding and situates each event in a larger context – helps us to see why philosophers often view narrativity as especially relevant to the constitution of an individual's identity. An individual's sense of her own identity also embodies understanding and enables her to situate the particular incidents and events of her life in a larger context.

6.2   The Self-Narrative View

As we saw in the previous section, all narratives have certain aspects in common. But there are also many ways in which narratives differ from one another. While some narratives are third-personal – as is the case with the reporter's story about last night's baseball game and the depiction of Dorothy's journey in *The Wizard of Oz* – other narratives are first-personal. A first-personal narrative is an individual's story about herself.

In developing narrative theories, philosophers have tended to focus on individuals' first-personal narratives. This version of the narrative approach – which has been defended by Schechtman, DeGrazia, and Lindemann – is what I will call the *self-narrative view*. The decision to focus on first-personal rather than third-personal narratives is perhaps unsurprising in light of the kind of issues raised by the characterization question. An answer to this question should help us make sense of an individual's identity; it should help us make sense of who she really is. Given that an individual has special access to her own mental states and actions and correspondingly is typically (if not always) especially authoritative about her own identity, narratives from the first-person perspective would seem to be particularly well suited to this task.

As we saw in the previous section, there are many different ways to convey information and depict events. Some of these ways are narrative in nature, while some of them are not. Likewise, there are many different ways for a being to organize its experiences. According to the self-narrative view, however, persons are distinctive in doing so by weaving stories of their lives, i.e., by creating self-narratives. Schechtman is particularly explicit about this point. On her view, persons are essentially self-creating creatures. In constituting one's narrative, one thereby comes to constitute one's self (Schechtman 1996, 94). In line with the general features of narrativity that we saw above, the process of constituting one's narrative requires more than simply listing the events of one's life sequentially. Rather, it is an active process of unification. While a person's narrative need not achieve perfect consistency, and while it need not have an overarching theme, the process of integrating distinct events together helps to make sense of them. It gives them a degree of coherence and intelligibility – indeed, it gives them meaning – that they otherwise would have lacked. A narrative understanding of identity is thus holistic. When an individual's self-conception is narrative in nature she understands and interprets her experiences against the background of the overall story of her life that imbues such experiences with their significance.

How such stories are constructed will undoubtedly vary greatly from person to person. Some will be more explicit than others, some more detailed, some more aspirational, some more cautious. A great variety of factors – gender, race, nationality, sexual orientation, political affiliation, family role, profession, hobbies, and so on – can play an organizing role in one's self-narrative. Consider Barbara Adams, an Arkansas woman and die-hard *Star Trek* fan committed to living her life according to the ideals espoused by the show. Adams had her five minutes of fame in the mid-1990s when she was selected for jury service on a high-profile trial and reported to court each day wearing a Starfleet uniform complete with a plastic phaser, tricorder, and communicator pin. (She was also subsequently featured in the documentary *Trekkies*.) At the time of the trial, Adams had been employed for a decade by a printing company. At her request, her colleagues addressed her as "Commander," consonant with her rank of lieutenant commander in a local *Star Trek* fan club. She could often be seen wearing her uniform around town. As she noted in a letter posted to the website Trekdoc.com:

> I've been a *Star Trek* fan as long as I can remember. I was two when it premiered, and I always remember seeing *Star Trek* while I was growing up in Brooklyn, NY. The positive future, our planet working with a league of other planets, and the intelligence and ideals that Gene Roddenberry and crew cleverly weaved into the plots...made it something that I could embrace for our future.

Adams has deliberately and self-consciously developed a self-narrative organized around her love of *Star Trek*. Her fandom affects not only how she lives her life but also her sense of who she is.

Proponents of the self-narrative theory do not agree with each other on all of the details of the theory. For example, while Schechtman insists that an individual's identity-constituting narrative must have a conventional, linear structure, Lindemann disagrees. On her view, an individual's identity is unlikely to be constituted by a single overarching story but rather by a network of many such stories, not all of which fit together in linear fashion. Another difference among proponents of the self-narrative theory arises from their assessment of the role that other people can play in constituting an individual's identity. Schechtman and DeGrazia focus almost exclusively on an individual's self-conception, but Lindemann contends that third-personal narratives can play a significant role in the constitution of an individual's identity. On her view, "identities are not simply a matter of how we experience our own lives, but also of how others see us" (Lindemann 2001, 81).

In defense of this claim, Lindemann asks us to consider a woman – I'll call her Cheryl – who sees herself as a skilled office manager, an indispensable asset to the company she works for. Unfortunately, the new management team considers her to be an outdated relic of a former era who ought to be guided into retirement. Faced with this perception from others, can Cheryl keep her own sense of herself in place? As Lindemann argues, since management has the power to fire Cheryl and thereby deny her a professional outlet in which to express her capabilities, their sense of her dictates the identities that are open to her. Even if Cheryl's professional commitments play a central role in her identity-constituting narrative, the opinions of others may preclude her from incorporating these commitments into her ongoing story of herself. Responding to this case, DeGrazia notes that, whatever management thinks of Cheryl and whatever steps they take to force her from the workplace, it can still be the case that she *is* a skilled worker and that she continues to regard herself as such (DeGrazia 2005, 87). The narratives of others cannot override my own self-narrative by fiat.

Yet even if DeGrazia is right that other people's stories cannot cancel out my own story, it seems plausible that other people's stories about me can influence my own story about myself, perhaps significantly so. Depending on how such influences are to be understood, this point can be taken in two different ways, either as a refinement of the self-narrative theory or as a rejection of it. Thane Plantikow, who seems to fall into the latter category, argues that third-person contributions play a critical role in the construction of identity-constituting narratives. On this view, such narratives should be seen not as autobiographical but as *co-autobiographical* (Plantikow 2008, 93). Alternatively, we might view the influence of third-person contributions in such a way that the identity-constituting narrative is still appropriately viewed as a *self*-narrative. Though such contributions might affect – perhaps even fundamentally so – an individual's own story about herself, it should still be seen as *her* story.

At this point, however, the natural objection is that once we think about the contrasts and connections between first- and third-personal narratives about an individual, we see that the two might conflict with one another. Surely people can be mistaken – perhaps even deeply mistaken – about themselves. Some individuals fancy themselves to be Napoleon, or to be the victim of a complex government conspiracy, or to have been abducted by aliens. But even apart from individuals who are deeply delusional in these ways, people may simply have seriously distorted conceptions of themselves. Consider a Wall Street banker who has for years been engaged in a ruthless pursuit of career advancement and personal wealth – let's call her Avery. And suppose that, by dint of careful editing and selective attention in the weaving of her story, Avery comes to see herself as a compassionate woman who has been an attentive mother to her kids. She focuses on the birthday presents she's bought rather than the birthday parties she's missed; she remembers clapping loudly at her son's performance in the school play but manages to ignore the fact that she'd arrived late to the show; her recollection of the family vacation in Hawaii excludes the fact that she spent most of the trip on her phone or her laptop. Avery presents us with a person whose self-narrative is out of step with the truth about who she really is. Though our stories about ourselves might change us in various ways – perhaps by providing us with aspirational pictures of ourselves that we aim to live up to – it nonetheless seems that the mere construction of a story cannot by itself make a person into someone she is not.

One way to guard against the problems arising from mistaken first-person narratives would be to develop the narrative theory in terms of third-personal, objective narratives instead. On this kind of view, which we might call the *objective-narrative view*, we would define what makes a person who she is not in terms of the narrative that she herself has constructed but rather in terms of a narrative from what we might think of as a God's eye view. Interestingly, such a view has not attracted adherents. The worry that we've been considering has not convinced self-narrative theorists to abandon their first-personal approach. From their perspective, addressing the characterization question from a purely objective point of view undermines the very spirit in which the question was asked in the first place. Issues of characterization are essentially first-personal in nature – it's the sort of question one asks by saying, "Who am I, really?" DeGrazia, whose own version of the self-narrative theory closely aligns with the one developed by Schechtman, notes that "only an answer that favors the first-person standpoint does justice to such a first-person question" (DeGrazia 2005, 84).

For this reason, DeGrazia himself opts for a framework in which one is the person who is *realistically* described by one's self-narrative. This allows for a balance between the objective and the subjective perspectives that protects against cases like Avery's while still privileging the first-personal point of view. Schechtman utilizes a similar strategy. In particular, her theory incorporates two constraints on what counts as an identity-constituting narrative. 2 Constraints

First, such narratives must be "capable of local articulation" – a person "should be able to explain why he does what he does, believes what he believes, and feels what he feels" (Schechtman 1996, 114). This is what Schechtman calls the *articulation constraint.* Importantly, this constraint does not require that the narrative must ever actually be articulated. We often do not explicitly lay out our own narratives, either to ourselves or to others. Rather, what the articulation constraint requires is only that we *could* provide an appropriate explanation or articulation if we were prompted to do so.

Second, such narratives must "fundamentally cohere with reality" (Schechtman 1996, 119). This is what Schechtman calls the *reality constraint.* For a narrative to cohere with reality in the relevant sense, it need not be completely accurate in every respect. A story can contain minor factual errors while still cohering with the basic contours of reality. What is precluded, however, is the inclusion of wildly false claims or a clearly inaccurate view of the world. As Schechtman summarizes it:

> An individual constitutes herself as a person by coming to organize her experience in a narrative self-conception of the appropriate form.... "Appropriate form" is not something determined arbitrarily, but rather something that comes out

of the complex lifestyles and social interactions definitive of personhood. The kind of narrative required is one that makes this lifestyle and set of interactions possible, and this involves, among other things, the demand that a person draw the limits of himself at essentially the same place that others do. (Schechtman 1996, 135)

6.3   The Case in Favor

The discussion of the previous section has fleshed out our understanding of the narrative theory of personal identity, and, in particular, the self-narrative version of this theory that has dominated philosophical discussion. But, while the previous section may have helped us to see some of the motivations in favor of the narrative theory, and while we've seen that the notion of narrativity seems to flow directly from the notion of identity at issue in the characterization question, we have not yet considered directly or in detail the case in support of this theory. That is the task of this section.

One consideration in favor of the self-narrative theory comes from its ability to make sense of the significant role that stories have traditionally played in human society. We are told stories from the earliest days of our childhood, and throughout our lives we turn to them for entertainment, for comfort, and for edification. We compare people to the fictional characters we've grown up with, and we compare events to familiar fictional plotlines. As Lindemann notes, we see both ourselves and others "in terms of the plot templates and character types we've known all our lives" (Lindemann 2001, 83). It's from stories that we learn about the human condition, and, correspondingly, stories shape our moral sensibilities. Stories also help us to be dreamers, to embrace the possibilities that the world offers us. The narrative theory helps us make sense of why stories have such deep resonance for us: our own lives are stories, and we ourselves are characters in them.

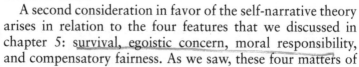

A second consideration in favor of the self-narrative theory arises in relation to the four features that we discussed in chapter 5: survival, egoistic concern, moral responsibility, and compensatory fairness. As we saw, these four matters of practical concern seem to have particularly deep-seated connections to theories of personal identity. Now that we have sketched the basic shape of the self-narrative view, we can see how it promises to account for these four features:

- We can explain my future <u>survival in terms of the continuation of my self-narrative</u>. Only when future experiences will be mine does it make sense for me to rationally anticipate them, and what it means for such future experiences to be mine is that they can be coherently and meaningfully incorporated into the story of my life. *Survival*

- <u>My concern for the future can be explained as a concern for myself as a</u> whole, as a continuing character in a particular life story. As David Shoemaker usefully puts it, we can explain this concern in terms of the fact that I'm "an extended narrative ego"; since my narrative is being constantly extended into the future, "my concern is *global*, a concern for the whole self I'm creating via this story, the whole self whose various parts are *mine*" (Shoemaker 2012). *egative concern*

- On the narrative theory, <u>what makes some past action *mine* is its incorporation into my own self-narrative</u>. Such incorporation helps to explain why I should be morally responsible for those actions. As parts of my narrative, such actions both cohere with and flow from my other experiences, values, beliefs, and so on. *moral resp*

- Likewise, when two experiences are <u>connected by being part of the same story</u> – when they are united in this coherent way – it seems plausible to think that one could fairly offset the other. Just as events that happen in disparate chapters of a book are connected to one another by the role they play in the story as a whole, a person's disparate experiences are connected by the role they play in her self-narrative as a whole. In compensating for a burden, a benefit can *redeem* it, thereby providing meaning to her overall self-narrative. *Compensating lines*

Proponents of the self-narrative view take its ability to offer these plausible explanations as a key point in its favor. Moreover, on their view, the explanations offered by the self-narrative view are superior to the kinds of explanations offered by theories of numerical identity. The case for this superiority derives in large part from the fact that the narrative theory takes a holistic approach to identity. Like the psychological theory, the self-narrative view assigns importance to sameness of consciousness. But, unlike the psychological theory, the self-narrative view sees sameness of consciousness not in terms of connections between temporally distant person stages but rather in terms of sameness of identity-constituting narrative.

As Schechtman notes, proponents of theories of numerical identity tend to offer various metaphors for their views. A further fact theorist might think of a person's identity through time on analogy with a string of beads. The string represents the unanalyzable fact of the person's identity – her Cartesian ego, perhaps, or her immaterial soul – while the beads represent her various experiences. Both the psychological theorist and the physical theorist might think of a person's identity through time on analogy with a river. Just as a river can be the same river over time even while the water that flows through it constantly changes, so too can a person be the same person over time even while the psychological or physical parts constantly change. In contrast to both of these metaphors, the self-narrative view might be thought of on analogy with a pot of soup. The soup contains many different ingredients, and as they blend together, an overall flavor emerges that is something over and above any one of them individually. Likewise, as an individual's various experiences blend together, an overall narrative is constituted that is something over and above any one of them individually. (See Schechtman 1996, 144.)

A third advantage of the self-narrative view comes from its ability to address various identity-related issues that are largely unaddressed by theories of numerical identity. Consider, for example, these real-life examples of first-person reflections on personal identity:

> I am a Canadian of Caribbean descent; my mother is from Barbados (my father is from England). I have a white face; and truth be told, a white body too. The fact is, however, that I am Black. How do I know? My mother told me so. (Baylis 2003, 143)

I've known all my life that I am a girl. I remember arguing enthusiastically as a child that I was not, in fact, the boy that people kept thinking I was. I have at various points in my life attempted to be the boy that everybody in my life seemed to want me to be. It never quite worked out. I came to terms with this several years ago, embraced my own identity and transitioned for the final time. (Hardie 2006, 122)

In my computer mediated worlds, the self is multiple, fluid, and constituted in interaction with machine connections; it is made and transformed by language... And in the machine-generated world of MUDs [Multi-User Domains], I meet characters who put me in a new relationship with my own identity. ... A MUD can become a context for discovering who one is and wishes to be. In this way, the games are laboratories for the construction of identity. (Turkle 1995, 15, 185)

These sorts of facts – facts about our racial and gender identities, or facts about our online identities – don't seem like issues that can be adequately handled by theories of reidentification. And there are many other kinds of examples we could introduce. To take just one, consider the fact that survivors of sexual assault or other deeply traumatic experiences claim that they are no longer the same person afterward. (See, e.g., Brison 2002, 44.) This claim seems to refer to a different kind of identity from numerical identity. All of these examples thus suggest that there are aspects of personal identity that require a different philosophical apparatus. In focusing on an individual's self-conception, the self-narrative theory seems well positioned to provide such an apparatus.

Many philosophers working on issues relating to gender and racial identity explicitly adopt a narrative framework. In a discussion of transitions from one sex or gender to another, Canadian philosopher Christine Overall argues that we develop our gender identities "by, in effect, creating the continuing narrative of our lives" (Overall 2009, 21). As she goes on to argue, nontrans people constitute their own gender identities by virtue of an ongoing narrative project derived from their original gender assignment. In contrast, trans people constitute their own gender identities by virtue of an ongoing narrative that resists their original gender assignment. Canadian philosopher Françoise Baylis, author of the passage quoted above about racial identity, also makes the connection to narrativity explicit: "My life is a collection of stories (mine and those of significant others) that tells me where I am from, where I have been and where I am going" (Baylis 2003, 145). From a very young age, Baylis deliberately incorporated her racial identity into her own self-narrative, something that wasn't always easy. She also had to work in all sorts of different ways to be sure that others saw her as she saw herself. As she explains, "Building a Black identity is hard work when you have white skin" (Baylis 2003, 144).

In some recent work, Schechtman has applied the narrative framework specifically to questions of online identity. In her view, the self-narrative view can help us to understand the role that an individual's online avatar can play in her identity. Consider the virtual world of Second Life, an online community which launched in 2003. After 10 years, it had more than 36 million subscribers. In signing up for the service, a person creates an avatar that allows her to interact with other subscribers' avatars within the virtual world. Subscribers control almost everything about their avatars: name, gender, physical appearance, occupation, and so on. But how should we understand the relationship between a subscriber and her avatar? In Schechtman's view, there are many instances in which a subscriber's narrative and her avatar's narrative – though distinct – are best understood as "parts of a single, broader person-narrative":

> sometimes the RL [real-life] narrative of the user and the SL [Second Life] narrative of the avatar are, as it were, subplots in the more comprehensive narrative of the resident, a person who lives sometimes in RL and sometimes in SL. Both sets of adventures are part of the same life because, although distinguishable sub-narratives, they impact each other along the most fundamental dimensions of narrative interaction. (Schechtman 2012, 341)

As Schechtman herself admits, the details need to be worked out further. To give just one example, what happens when an individual has two distinct avatars whose narratives are in various ways in tension with one another? But when it comes to questions about online identity – like questions of racial, gender, and cultural identity – the self-narrative theory seems particularly apt.

Bioethical debates provide another set of contexts in which narrative theories of identity have proved relevant. One such issue concerns the moral permissibility of various enhancement technologies, from drug therapies to genetic interventions. Suppose, for example, that genetic manipulation could dramatically reduce a person's need for sleep, or dramatically increase her memory capacity. Worries about such technologies are often expressed in identity-related terms. For example, in a 2003 report called *Beyond Therapy*, the President's Commission on Bioethics worried that "In seeking by these means to be better than we are or to like ourselves better than we do, we risk 'turning into someone else,' confounding the identity we have acquired through natural gift cultivated by genuinely lived experiences, alone and with others." Whether or not such concern is ultimately justified, it seems clear that the sense of identity in question is better understood in narrative rather than numerical terms. One does not become a numerically distinct person through these genetic interventions, though one might dramatically reshape one's self-narrative.

Despite these advantages, however, it's probably not surprising that philosophers disagree about whether the self-narrative view provides an adequate answer to the characterization question. Though criticisms come from various sources, in the next section we will focus on three of the most central sorts of objections. First, worries arise from the inclusion of a reality constraint. Second, some philosophers deny that the narrative theory accurately and universally captures their lived experiences, i.e., they deny that constructing a narrative is essential to our lives as persons. Third, even if it's true that narrative self-construction does play an essential role in our lives as persons, further worries arise from the fact that narrative identity cannot be understood without presupposing numerical identity.

6.4 The Case Against

Above, we saw that self-narrative theorists tend to employ some sort of reality constraint in an attempt to guard against counterexamples arising from individuals whose self-narratives are drastically out of step with the objective facts about their lives. In doing so, however, the self-narrative theorists open themselves up to further criticism. Plantikow, for example, argues that the inclusion of a reality constraint prevents self-narrative theories from dealing adequately with the personal identity of individuals with psychiatric disorders. Consider someone who suffers from paranoia and takes herself to be the target of a widespread conspiracy. When she sees people in dark blue suits on the street, she thinks that they're following her. When she hears static while listening to the radio, she takes it as evidence that she's being constantly monitored. Her beliefs about herself and about what's going on around her are false. Her self-narrative violates the reality constraint. In Plantikow's view, however, the fact of this violation may itself be relevant to who she really is: "I believe that we should wonder which is more important to identity constitution: the fact that the paranoiac is wrong, so to speak, or the fact that she believes she is right. Schechtman would have us neglect the latter in light of the former" (Plantikow 2008, 98).

Likewise, when considering someone with the delusion that he's Napoleon, it might be relevant that the individual takes himself to be Napoleon rather than, say, Elvis Presley. As Plantikow notes, if no delusional claims are identity-constituting, then we have no way to distinguish one such claim from another in terms of its impact on identity (Plantikow 2008, 99). Australian philosopher Steve Matthews has raised concerns along similar lines, arguing that the falsity of an individual's memories should not in itself exclude them from playing an identity-constituting role: "if someone has false memories of (say) walking on the Moon, do we say these states are not relevant to this person's identity? Surely we want to say it is part of this person's identity that he has these false memories" (Matthews 1998, 82–3). Examples of this sort raise the more general concern that evaluating self-narratives according to the reality constraint might conceal or obscure certain important facts about an individual's identity.

The narrative theorist is thus faced with a dilemma. On the one hand, the sorts of concerns raised by Plantikow and

Matthews seem important. On the other hand, it is hard to see how a self-narrative theory could be plausible absent any condition that provides some real-world check on an individual's narrative. Thus, unless there is some way to elaborate this condition that avoids these sorts of problems, the plausibility of the self-narrative theory would be called into doubt.

Unlike this first worry, which concerns a particular aspect of the self-narrative view, the second objection we will consider – which is one of the primary sources of opposition to the view – strikes right at the heart of the theory. The problem arises from apparent counterexamples to the view, i.e., from the existence of people – fully competent adult human beings – who claim not to experience any narrative structure in their lives. As we have seen, proponents of the self-narrative theory take the construction of a self-narrative as central to one's having an identity in the sense of the characterization question, and, indeed, as central to personhood. Such proponents admit that people can differ considerably from one another in terms of how explicitly developed their self-narratives are. Some people might self-consciously reflect on their overall sense of themselves on a daily basis. Others might rarely if ever subject themselves to this kind of inner scrutiny. But even while recognizing that these sorts of differences exist, narrative theorists are nonetheless committed to a universal claim. As DeGrazia says, "Despite individual variations, every person has a mental autobiography" (DeGrazia 2005, 81). The existence of non-narrative people would thus pose a significant challenge to the self-narrative theory.

Perhaps the most prominent expression of this challenge comes from the work of Galen Strawson, a British philosopher who denies that his own life exhibits narrativity, i.e., who denies that he has the kind of mental autobiography referenced by DeGrazia. Strawson's discussion centers on the distinction between two types of people – those he calls *diachronics* and those he calls *episodics.* Someone who experiences life as a diachronic thinks of herself as someone who was there in the past (both the immediate and the further past) and who will be there in the future (again, both the immediate and the further future). Thinking of herself this way means that she considers herself to be a continuing and persisting entity through a relatively long stretch of time. In contrast, someone who experiences life as an episodic does not think of herself – when considering herself as a *self* – as a continuing and persisting entity through a relatively long stretch of time. She has little or no sense that she is the self who was there in the further past or the one who will be there in the further future. This is not to say that she soon expects to experience bodily death. As an episodic, she can accept that the human being that she is has been around a long time and may continue to be around for a long time. Rather, it's the *self* that she is that is thought of in episodic terms.

As Strawson notes, episodics and diachronics tend to have trouble understanding each other's basic perspectives. To a diachronic, an episodic outlook may look "chilling, empty and deficient." To an episodic, a diachronic outlook may look "excessively self-concerned" and "inauthentically second-order" (Strawson 2004, 431). Strawson thus attempts to elucidate more carefully what his own experience is like as an episodic:

> I have a past, like any human being, and I know perfectly well that I have a past. I have a respectable amount of factual knowledge about it, and I also remember some of my past experiences "from the inside," as philosophers say. And yet I have absolutely no sense of my life as a narrative with form, or indeed as a narrative without form. Absolutely none. Nor do I have any great or special interest in my past. Nor do I have a great deal of concern for my future. (Strawson 2004, 433)

Strawson also claims that he is not the only one to take an episodic perspective. In his view, the writings of a vast array of people – people as varied as the author Virginia Woolf, the poet Emily Dickinson, and the singer/songwriter Bob Dylan – reveal episodic outlooks.

While it may be open to a diachronic to frame his life either narratively or non-narratively, an episodic outlook is inconsistent with the kind of narrativity that narrative theorists claim is central to personal identity. (Insofar as an episodic participates in any activity that involves a sequence of steps, there may be some narrativity in his life – if, say, a narrative is required for the mundane act of making dinner or doing laundry – but any such narrativity would be narrativity only in a trivial sense of the term.) Having put himself forward as an example of an episodic, then, Strawson concludes that the self-narrative approach must be false. His basic line of criticism can be summarized in the following simple argument:

1. If the self-narrative theory is true, then all persons structure their experiences in narrative form.
2. I (Galen Strawson) am a person.
3. I (Galen Strawson) do not structure my experiences in narrative form.
4. Thus, it's not the case that all persons structure their experiences in narrative form.
5. Thus, the self-narrative theory is false.

The universality of the self-narrative theory is also called into question by people who simply live their life as it comes and who rarely if ever stop to self-consciously reflect on what's happening to them. Even people who are more future-oriented might only very occasionally stop to attempt to make sense of their lives as a whole. Though life may present them with moments in which they take a self-reflective turn, such moments might be too few and far-between to make it the case that any kind of overarching narrative plays a role in shaping their experience. More to the point, it's not clear that self-reflection in and of itself is enough to count as organizing one's life in narrative form. British philosopher Samantha Vice has developed the point as follows: consider how often you have stopped to tell yourself your autobiography, or how often you try to detect overall patterns and try to evaluate your behavior in light of some larger significance. She predicts that for most of us this happens only rarely and, more importantly, only retrospectively. On her view, the project of giving our lives form and meaning is not something that we tend to do in the heat of the moment. It is not a project that seems in any way to impact us as we go about our daily lives (Vice 2003, 107).

What might a self-narrative theorist say in response? One possible strategy would be to reorient the theory as a prescriptive rather than a descriptive view. If the narrative view aims to describe identity in the sense of the characterization question, then the existence of non-narrative individuals like

Strawson – non-narrative *persons* – poses a serious threat. But if, instead, the narrative view aims to offer a prescriptive view – to offer a theory of what accounts for an individual's flourishing, or what it is for an individual to live a good life – then the threat from the existence of episodic individuals can be deflected.

Typically, however, this has not been the strategy employed by narrative theorists. Instead, they have attempted to reinterpret Strawson's self-reports to show that he is wrong in thinking that they are incompatible with narrativity, i.e., they have attempted to deny the third premise of the argument above. This general strategy of response – the denial of premise 3 – is a tricky business. For such a strategy to succeed, it would not be enough to show merely that the events of Strawson's life *could be* conceived along narrative lines. While that may be true, it does not show that his experiences are *actually* structured narratively; it does not show that he has in any way created a self-narrative. This points to the very delicate balance that must be struck in articulating an adequate conception of narrativity. On the one hand, one doesn't want to end up with a conception of narrativity that is so weak as to be trivial or empty. On the other hand, one needs to be able to defend against counterexamples like Strawson.

In attempting to strike this balance, Schechtman points out that there is a potential continuum among narrative theories ranging from those that require a very strong degree of narrativity to those that require a considerably weaker degree of narrativity. Situating her own view somewhere in the middle, Schechtman notes that, while the conception of narrative that she employs requires more than merely ordering one's experiences chronologically, it does not require anything as demanding as conformity to a distinct literary genre, or the construction of a well-defined plot arc, or a synthesis in terms of a unifying theme (Schechtman 2007, 163). According to Schechtman, her middle-of-the-road position is compatible with most of what Strawson reports about his own outlook. In particular, the relations he acknowledges as holding within his human existence are themselves indicative of narrativity.

But Strawson does not merely claim that he is an episodic. He also explicitly denies that he frames *any* kind of narrative about his existence. In denying premise 3, a narrative theorist like Schechtman is thus rejecting Strawson's own self-report: though he does not believe himself to have a narrative outlook, he is mistaken about the structure of his own experiences. Such a claim, however, is rather unappealing. While we can be wrong about all sorts of things, it is troubling to think that we can be wrong about what we experience. How can someone else know better than I do what my experience is like? Narrative theorists thus seem to be making a mistake of overgeneralization. Though they take themselves to be describing the experiences of *all* persons, to be offering a general theory of personal identity, in fact they are just describing how they themselves experience life. (See Strawson 2004, 439.)

Ultimately, however, even if the narrative theorists can adequately respond to these first two challenges to their view, there is a third challenge with which they are confronted. The problem arises from the fact that narrative identity cannot be understand in isolation from numerical identity. Consider again the delusional individual – let's call him Mason – who thinks that he is Napoleon and frames his self-narrative accordingly. In explaining why his narrative cannot be identity-constituting – in explaining why it violates Schechtman's reality constraint – the narrative theorist must make use of the fact that Mason is not Napoleon – that is, that they are numerically distinct people. Narrative identity thus presupposes numerical identity.

This fact in itself need not trouble the narrative theorist. Indeed, it is something such theorists have typically acknowledged explicitly in the development of their theories. (See, e.g., DeGrazia 2005, 114.) But it leads to a deeper issue. Recall that the case for the narrative theory relies in large part on its ability to account for certain facts about our existence that are either neglected, or not well addressed, by theories of numerical identity, facts about certain practical concerns like the four features, say, or facts about our racial and gender identities. Once we realize that the narrative theory presupposes numerical identity, however, the case for the narrative theory is somewhat undercut. It is no longer clear that it is narrative identity per se that is doing the relevant theoretical work. Insofar as numerical identity underlies narrative identity, it might be argued that the facts of numerical identity are indeed relevant to these issues as well. The proponent of the narrative theory is thus faced with a more difficult task than we might have realized: in showing that the narrative theory can account for these various matters, she must also show that it does so independent of its reliance on facts about numerical identity.

Even more problematically, the fact that narrative identity presupposes numerical identity highlights a tension at the heart of the self-narrative view. According to such a view, an individual constitutes herself as a person by framing her life in narrative terms. But this means that the individual pre-exists any such framing – only someone who already exists can be responsible for shaping her life in narrative terms. (See, e.g., Rudd 2005 and Vollmer 2005.) Perhaps the narrative theorist will say that one does not yet exist *as a person* until one adopts a narrative outlook. But because persons are meant to be precisely the sort of beings who engage in narrative framing, this wouldn't be a very satisfying response.

6.5   Summing Up

We turned to the narrative theory as an attempt to answer a question – "Who am I, really?" – that was left unanswered by theories of numerical identity. As we have seen, the notion of narrativity proves relevant to many facts about our identities, facts about how we *self-identify*, which theories of numerical identity have largely tended to ignore. Moreover, the narrative theory accounts nicely for many of our practical concerns, as well as for the importance of stories in our lives. Ultimately, however, there are some objections to it that look difficult to overcome.

Interestingly, there is in the philosophical literature no real alternative to the narrative theory. Thus, even if the theory seems lacking in some respects, it is difficult to see what our options are for doing better. One possibility might be to return to theories of numerical identity. Though they have not yet been put to use in addressing many of the issues we encountered in this chapter, that does not mean that we couldn't find some way to do so. Moreover, insofar as some philosophers have worried about whether the characterization question itself collapses into the reidentification question (as we saw in the previous chapter), it would seem worthwhile to explore how theories of numerical identity might be brought to bear on the sorts of issues we've explored in this chapter.

As our discussion throughout this book demonstrates, questions about persons and personal identity typically do not have easy answers. Given that these questions are so central to who we are – given that they concern facts about our very nature and existence in the world – it might be surprising that they are so hard to sort out. But it's precisely because these issues hit so close to home that it seems well worth our continuing to try. Though the discussion of the book is now at a close, I hope that you will continue to ponder these issues as you make your way through life. Certainly they will be relevant to many of the situations that you'll encounter – whether it's reidentifying friends that you haven't seen for quite a while, or dealing with aging relatives with dementia, or contemplating the use of various drug therapies that have dramatic psychological and physical effects. And who knows – one day you may have to decide whether to step onto a transporter, or whether to upload your consciousness to a computer, or whether to accept a surgeon's offer to transplant your brain into another body.

Further Reading

For developments of the self-narrative view beyond those discussed in this chapter, see Dennett (1992) and Bruner (1990). Shoemaker (2009) provides a useful overview of the narrative theory as well as a careful discussion of its advantages and disadvantages. For further discussion of whether and how one can develop a coherent conception of narrativity that is appropriately balanced between weak and strong senses of the term, see Christman (2004).

Shrage (2009) is a useful collection of papers relating to sex reassignment and personal identity. For discussion of the interplay between narrativity and racial identity, see Appiah (1990). Velleman (2008) and Wolfendale (2007) both provide interesting explorations related to the issue of online identity. Though not a philosophical text, Turkle (1995) nonetheless provides very useful fodder for philosophical engagement with this issue. The relationship between bioethical concerns and the self-narrative theory is explored in detail in DeGrazia (2005, esp. chs. 4–7). Brison (2002) explores the importance of self-narrative in recovering from trauma.

The 2006 movie *Stranger than Fiction* directed by Marc Forster provides a fanciful exploration of the role of narrativity in shaping our sense of self. Starring Will Ferrell as an IRS auditor, the film explores what happens when he "suddenly finds himself the subject of narration only he can hear: narration that begins to affect his entire life, from his work, to his love-interest, to his death" (www.imdb.com/title/tt0420223). David Fincher's *Fight Club* is also relevant to the issues of this chapter, and, more generally, to the issues in the book as a whole.

Bibliography

Adams, Douglas. 1979. *The Hitchhiker's Guide to the Galaxy*. Pocket Books.

American Psychiatric Association. 2013. *Diagnostic and Statistical Manual of Mental Disorders* (5th edition). American Psychiatric Publishing.

Appiah, Anthony. 1990. " 'But Would That Still Be Me?' Notes on Gender, 'Race,' Ethnicity, as Sources of 'Identity.' " *The Journal of Philosophy* 87 (10): 493–9.

Baker, Lynne Rudder. 2012. "Personal Identity: A Not-So-Simple Simple View." In Matthias Stefan, ed., *Personal Identity: Simple or Complex*. Cambridge University Press. 179–91.

Baker, Lynne Rudder. 2007. "Persons and Other Things." *Journal of Consciousness Studies* 14: 17–36.

Baylis, Françoise. 2003. "Black As Me: Narrative Identity." *Developing World Bioethics* 3: 142–50.

Beauchamp, Tom L. 1999. "The Failure of Theories of Personhood." *Kennedy Institute of Ethics Journal* 9: 309–24.

Blatti, Stephan. 2014. "Animalism." *Stanford Encyclopedia of Philosophy*. Available at http://plato.stanford.edu/archives/sum2014/entries/animalism.

Boethius, Anicius Manlius Severinus. 1918. *The Theological Tractates and The Consolation of Philosophy*, translated by H. F. Stewart and E. K. Rand. Harvard University Press.

Bourget, David, and David Chalmers. 2014. "What Do Philosophers Believe?" *Philosophical Studies* 170: 465–500.

Braude, Stephen. 1991. *First Person Plural: Multiple Personality and the Philosophy of Mind*. Routledge.

Brison, Susan. 2002. *Aftermath: Violence and the Remaking of a Self*. Princeton University Press.

Bruner, Jerome. 1990. *Acts of Meaning*. Harvard University Press.

Butler, Joseph. 1736. "Of Personal Identity." Reprinted in Perry 2008, 99–105.

Cavalieri, Paola, and Peter Singer, eds. 1993. *The Great Ape Project*. St. Martin's Griffin.

Chisholm, Roderick. 1977. *Person and Object*. Open Court Publishing Company.

Christman, John P. 2004. "Narrative Unity as a Condition of Personhood." *Metaphilosophy* 35: 695–713.

Cohen, Carl. 1986. "The Case for the Use of Animals in Biomedical Research." *The New England Journal of Medicine* 315: 865–70.

Damasio, Antonio. 1994. *Descartes' Error: Emotion, Reason, and the Human Brain*. Avon Books.

DeGrazia, David. 2005. *Human Identity and Bioethics*. Cambridge University Press.

Dennett, Daniel. 1992. "The Self as a Center of Narrative Gravity." In F. S. Kessel, P. M. Cole, and D. L. Johnson, eds., *Self and Consciousness: Multiple Perspectives*. Erlbaum Associates. 103–15.

Dennett, Daniel. 1976. "Conditions of Personhood." In Rorty 1976, 175–96.

English, Jane. 2005. "Abortion and the Concept of a Person." *Canadian Journal of Philosophy* 5 (2): 233–43.

Feinberg, Joel, and Barbara Baum Levenbook. 1992. "Abortion." In Tom Regan, ed., *Matters of Life and Death* (3rd edition). McGraw-Hill. 195–213.

Francione, Gary. 1993. "Personhood, Property, and Legal Competence." In Cavalieri and Singer 1993, 248–57.

Frankfurt, Harry. 1976. "Identification and Externality." In Rorty 1976, 239–52.

Frankfurt, Harry. 1971. "Freedom of the Will and the Concept of a Person." *The Journal of Philosophy* 68: 5–20.

Gallup, G. G., Jr. 1970. "Chimpanzees: Self Recognition." *Science* 167: 86–7.

Gendler, Tamar Szabo. 2002. "Personal Identity and Thought Experiments." *The Philosophical Quarterly* 52: 34–54.

Hardie, Alaina. 2006. "It's a Long Way to the Top: Hierarchies of Legitimacy in Trans Communities." In Krista Scott-Dixon, ed., *Trans/forming Feminisms: Trans/Feminist Voices Speak Out*. Sumach Press. 122–30.

Herzing, Denise, and Thomas White. 1998. "Dolphins and the Question of Personhood." *Etica Animali* 9: 64–84.

Johnston, Mark. 1989. "Relativism and the Self." In Michael Krausz, ed., *Relativism: Interpretation and Confrontation*. University of Notre Dame Press. 441–72.

Kaplan, Justine. 1989. "Interview: Louis Herman." *Omni* 11: 76.

Kittay, Eva Feder. 2005. "At the Margins of Moral Personhood." *Ethics* 116: 100–31.

Korfmacher, Carsten. 2006. "Personal Identity." *Internet Encyclopedia of Philosophy*. Available at www.iep.utm.edu/person-i.

Kurzweil, Ray. 2005. *The Singularity is Near: When Humans Transcend Biology*. Penguin Books.

Lewis, David. 1976. "Survival and Identity." In Rorty 1976, 17–40.

Lindemann, Hilde. 2001. *Damaged Identities, Narrative Repair*. Cornell University Press. Originally published under the name "Hilde Lindemann Nelson."

Locke, John. 1689/1975. *An Essay Concerning Human Understanding*, edited with an introduction by Peter H. Nidditch. Oxford University Press.

Madell, Geoffrey. 1981. *The Identity of the Self*. Edinburgh University Press.

Martin, Raymond, and John Barresi, eds. 2003. *Personal Identity*. Blackwell Press.

Matthews, Steve. 1998. "Personal Identity, Multiple Personality Disorder, and Moral Personhood." *Philosophical Psychology* 11 (1): 67–88.

McMahan, Jeff. 2002. *The Ethics of Killing: Problems at the Margins of Life*. Oxford University Press.

Nagel, Thomas. 1986. *The View from Nowhere*. Oxford University Press.

Nagel, Thomas. 1971. "Brain Bisection and the Unity of Consciousness." *Synthese* 22: 396–413.

Noonan, Harold W. 2003. *Personal Identity* (2nd edition). Routledge.

Olson, Eric. 2003a. "An Argument for Animalism." In Martin and Barresi 2003, 318–34.

Olson, Eric. 2003b. "Was Jekyll Hyde?" *Philosophy and Phenomenological Research* 66: 328–48.

Olson, Eric. 1997. *The Human Animal: Personal Identity Without Psychology*. Oxford University Press.

Overall, Christine. 2009. "Sex/Gender Transitions and Life-Changing Aspirations." In Shrage 2009, 11–27.

Parfit, Derek. 1984. *Reasons and Persons*. Oxford University Press.

Patterson, Francine, and Wendy Gordon. 1993. "The Case for the Personhood of Gorillas." In Cavalieri and Singer 1993, 58–75.

Pepperberg, Irene Maxine. 2008. *Alex and Me*. Harper Press.

Pepperberg, Irene Maxine. 2002. *The Alex Studies: Cognitive and Communicative Abilities of Grey Parrots*. Harvard University Press.

Perry, John, ed. 2008. *Personal Identity (revised edition)*. University of California Press.

Perry, John. 1978. *A Dialogue on Personal Identity and Immortality*. Hackett Publishing Company.

Perry, John. 1976. "The Importance of Being Identical." In Rorty 1976, 67–90.

Perry, John. 1975. "Personal Identity, Memory, and the Problem of Circularity." In Perry 2008, 135–55.

Plantikow, Thane. 2008. "Surviving Personal Identity Theory: Recovering Interpretability." *Hypatia* 23: 90–109.

Prince, Morton. 1905. *The Dissociation of a Personality: A Biographical Study*. Longman's, Green, and Co.

Putnam, F. W. 1989. *Diagnosis and Treatment of Multiple Personality Disorder*. Guilford.

Radden, Jennifer. 1996. *Divided Minds and Successive Selves*. MIT Press.

Regan, Tom. 2004. *The Case for Animal Rights*. University of California Press.

Reid, Thomas. 1785. "Of Mr. Locke's Account of Our Personal Identity." Reprinted in Perry 2008, 113–18.

Reiss, Diane, and Lori Marino. 2001. "Mirror Self-recognition in the Bottlenose Dolphin: A Case of Cognitive Convergence." *Proceedings of the National Academy of Sciences* 98 (10): 5937–42.

Ricoeur, Paul. 1991. "Narrative Identity," translated by Mark S. Muldoon. *Philosophy Today* 35: 73–81.

Rorty, Amélie Oksenberg, ed. 1976. *The Identities of Persons*. University of California Press.

Ross, Colin A. 1994. *The Osiris Complex*. University of Toronto Press.

Rudd, Anthony J. 2005. "Narrative, Expression and Mental Substance." *Inquiry* 48 (5): 413–35.

Sacks, Oliver. 2007. "The Abyss." *The New Yorker*. Available at www.newyorker.com/magazine/2007/09/24/the-abyss.

Saks, Elyn. 2000. *Jekyll on Trial: Multiple Personality Disorder and Criminal Law*. New York University Press.

Schechtman, Marya. 2014. *Staying Alive: Personal Identity, Practical Concerns, and the Unity of a Life*. Oxford University Press.

Schechtman, Marya. 2012. "The Story of my (Second) Life: Virtual Worlds and Narrative Identity," *Philosophy & Technology* 25: 329–43.

Schechtman, Marya. 2007. "Stories, Lives, and Basic Survival: A Refinement and Defense of the Narrative View." *Royal Institute of Philosophy Supplements* 82: 155–78.

Schechtman, Marya. 1996. *The Constitution of Selves*. Cornell University Press.

Shoemaker, David. 2012. "Personal Identity and Ethics". *Stanford Encyclopedia of Philosophy* Available at http://plato.stanford.edu/archives/spr2014/entries/identity-ethics/.

Shoemaker, David. 2009. *Personal Identity and Ethics*. Broadview Press.

Shoemaker, Sydney. 1984. "Personal Identity: A Materialist's Account." In Sydney Shoemaker and Richard Swinburne, *Personal Identity*. Blackwell.

Shrage, Laurie J., ed. 2009. *"You've Changed": Sex Reassignment and Personal Identity*. Oxford University Press.

Sider, Theodore. 2001. *Four Dimensionalism: An Ontology of Persistence and Time*. Oxford University Press.

Singer, Peter. 1975/1990. *Animal Liberation*. Avon Books.

Snowdon, Paul F. 1990 "Persons, Animals, and Ourselves." In Christopher Gill, ed., *The Person and the Human Mind: Issues in Ancient and Modern Philosophy*. Clarendon Press. 83–107.

Solum, Lawrence B. 2008. "Legal Personhood for Artificial Intelligences." *North Carolina Law Review* 70: 1231–87.

Stone, Christopher. 1972. "Should Trees Have Standing? Toward Legal Rights for Natural Objects." *Southern California Law Review* 45 (2): 450–501.

Strawson, Galen. 2004. "Against Narrativity." *Ratio* 17: 428–52.

Strawson, P. F. 1959. *Individuals: An Essay in Descriptive Metaphysics*. Routledge.

Swinburne, Richard. 1973–4. "Personal Identity." *Proceedings of the Aristotelian Society, New Series*, 74: 231–47.

Taylor, Charles. 1989. *Sources of the Self: The Making of the Modern Identity*. Harvard University Press.

Thomson, Judith Jarvis. 1997. "People and Their Bodies." In Jonathan Dancy, ed., *Reading Parfit*, Blackwell Publishers. 202–29.

Tooley, Michael. 1983. *Abortion and Infanticide*. Oxford University Press.

Tur, Richard. 1987. "The 'Person' in Law." In Arthur Peacocke and Grant Gillett, eds., *Persons and Personality: A Contemporary Inquiry*. Blackwell. 116–29.

Turkle, Sherry. 1995. *Life on the Screen: Identity in the Age of the Internet*. Simon and Schuster.

Unger, Peter. 1990. *Identity, Consciousness and Value*. Oxford University Press.

Velleman, J. David. 2008. "Bodies, Selves." *American Imago* 65 (3): 405–26.

Vice, Samantha. 2003. "Literature and the Narrative Self." *Philosophy* 78: 93–108.

Vollmer, Fred. 2005. "The Narrative Self." *Journal for the Theory of Social Behaviour* 35 (2): 189–205.

Warren, Mary Anne. 1997. *Moral Status*. Oxford University Press.

Warren, Mary Anne. 1973. "On the Moral and Legal Status of Abortion." *The Monist* 57 (1): 43–61.

White, Thomas. 2010. "Dolphin People." *The Philosopher's Magazine* 49: 36–43.

White, Thomas. 2007. *In Defense of Dolphins*. Blackwell Publishing.

Wilkes, Kathleen. 1988. *Real People: Personal Identity Without Thought Experiments*. Oxford University Press.

Williams, Bernard. 1973. *Problems of the Self*. Cambridge University Press.

Williams, Bernard. 1970. "The Self and the Future." *Philosophical Review* 79. Reprinted in Williams 1973, 46–63.

Williams, Bernard. 1960. "Personal Identity and Bodily Continuity – A Reply." *Analysis* 21. Reprinted in Williams 1973, 19–25.

Williams, Bernard. 1956–7. "Personal Identity and Individuation." *Proceedings of the Aristotelian Society* 57. Reprinted in Williams 1973, 1–18.

Wolfendale, Jessica. 2007. "My Avatar, My Self: Virtual Harm and Attachment." *Ethics and Information Technology* 9: 111–19.

Index

3   bt
1   HC
2   vb